Bescherelle

Anglais 5ᵉ

Niveaux A1+ ➜ A2 du CECRL

Sylvie Collard-Rebeyrolle
Agrégée de l'Université
Professeur au collège Paul Verlaine à Faulquemont (57)

Jeanne-France Bignaux
Agrégée de l'Université
Professeur au lycée Alfred Kastler à Cergy (95)

Wilfrid Rotgé
Agrégé de l'Université
Professeur de linguistique anglaise à l'université Paris Sorbonne

Hatier

@)) Le site www.bescherelle.com

Ce cahier te donne accès
au site **www.bescherelle.com**.

Tu y trouveras :

- tous les fichiers MP3
  associés à l'entraînement oral ;

- la BD enregistrée.

Conception graphique	**Anne Gallet**
Réalisation	**Nadine Aymard**
Illustrations	**Nathalie Dieterlé**
Suivi éditorial	**Barthélemy de Lesseps**

© Hatier, Paris, juin 2015   ISSN 2101-1249   ISBN 978-2-218-99166-0

Sommaire

Au centre du cahier :
- les corrigés de tous les exercices ;
- la BD *Nice to meet you, Robin Hood!*

@)) Sur le site www.bescherelle.com
tous les fichiers MP3 pour s'entraîner à l'oral

L'alphabet phonétique

Voyelles brèves		Voyelles longues	
/ɪ/	big, England	/iː/	beach, see
/e/	bed, pen	/ɑː/	car, father
/æ/	cat, hat	/ɔː/	walk, more
/ɒ/	dog, got	/uː/	two, moon
/ʊ/	good, book	/ɜː/	bird, work
/ʌ/	bus, does		
/ə/	gorilla, an		

Diphtongues		Consonnes	
/eɪ/	cake, mail	/θ/	thank, thing
/aɪ/	cry, five	/ð/	mother, this
/ɔɪ/	boy, toy	/z/	zebra, dogs
/əʊ/	hope, don't	/ʃ/	sugar, shoes
/aʊ/	brown, house	/ʒ/	beige, treasure
/ɪə/	year, here	/tʃ/	children, teacher
/eə/	hair, there	/dʒ/	job, jeans
/ʊə/	poor, sure	/ŋ/	English, singing
		/j/	yes, uniform

Le signe /'/ indique l'accent de mot.

Les abréviations

V	:	verbe
V-ing	:	verbe + -ing
pl.	:	pluriel
Ø	:	article zéro
≠	:	différent de
sb	:	somebody
qqn	:	quelqu'un
sth	:	something
qqch.	:	quelque chose
(GB)	:	anglais britannique
(US)	:	anglais américain

Les crochets [ ] signalent une précision grammaticale ou lexicale.

L'astérisque * indique les verbes irréguliers.

Mode d'emploi

Dans le cahier

● **Tout le programme en 24 chapitres et 110 exercices corrigés**

Dans les pages **grammaire** et **vocabulaire** :
• à gauche, les révisions des points clés ;
• à droite, les exercices (corrigés détachables au centre du cahier).

Dans les pages *Sounds, sounds, sounds…*, les exercices d'**entraînement à l'oral** avec un rappel de la règle si nécessaire.

● **Une BD à lire et à écouter :**
Nice to meet you, Robin Hood!

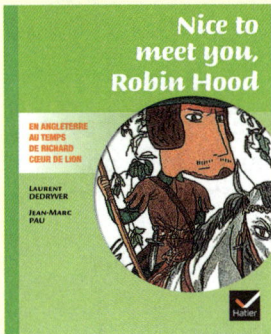

Cette BD, librement inspirée des aventures de Robin des Bois, nous emmène en Angleterre au temps de Richard Cœur de Lion.
26 épisodes à lire et à écouter,
avec un quiz pour vérifier qu'on a compris.

Sur le site www.bescherelle.com

Tous les fichiers MP3 associés à l'ouvrage en accès gratuit pour les utilisateurs du livre

@)) Les exercices d'entraînement **à l'oral**

@)) Les 26 épisodes de la **BD**

1 Les verbes **be** et **have**

| **Be** peut souvent se traduire par « être » et **have** par « avoir ».

✳ Le verbe **be**

● **Be** au présent

	I	he/she/it	we/you/they
affirmation	I'm (I am)	it's (it is)	we're (we are)
négation	I'm not (I am not)	he isn't (he is not)	you aren't (you are not)
interrogation	am I?	is it?	are they?

● **Be** au prétérit

	I/he/she/it	we/you/they
affirmation	I was	we were
négation	he wasn't (he was not)	you weren't (you were not)
interrogation	was it?	were they?

● On utilise parfois « avoir » en français là où on emploie **be** en anglais.

Li **is** twelve. I'm fourteen.
Li a douze ans. Moi, j'en ai quatorze.

I'm right and you're wrong.
J'ai raison et tu as tort.

I'm cold and hungry.
J'ai froid et faim.

● « Il y a » se dit « **there is** + nom au singulier » ou « **there are** + nom au pluriel ».

"There **is** a problem." "No, there **are** many problems."
« Il y a un problème. – Non, il y a beaucoup de problèmes. »

✳ Le verbe **have**

● Pour dire « avoir, posséder », on peut employer **have got** ou **have** seul. Quand **have** s'emploie seul pour dire « avoir », il se conjugue comme un verbe ordinaire, avec **do**.

	I/we/you/they	he/she/it
affirmation	You've got time. You have time. Tu as du temps.	She's got time. She has time. Elle a du temps.
négation	You haven't got time. You don't have time. Tu n'as pas de temps.	She hasn't got time. She doesn't have time. Elle n'a pas de temps.
interrogation	Have you got time? Do you have time? Est-ce que tu as du temps ?	Has she got time? Does she have time? Est-ce qu'elle a du temps ?

● Au prétérit, **have** n'a qu'une forme pour toutes les personnes : **had**. La négation et l'interrogation se forment avec **did**.

I **had** time.
J'avais du temps.

She **didn't have** time.
Elle n'avait pas de temps.

Did he **have** time?
Est-ce qu'il avait du temps?

Exercices

1 Choisis la forme qui convient.

1. Who .... cold?

    a. has   **b.** is   **c.** are   **d.** have got

2. Who .... cousins in Edinburgh?

    a. are   **b.** have   **c.** will be   **d.** has got

3. We .... enough time.

    a. don't have   **b.** haven't   **c.** has   **d.** are

4. We .... a house in New York, we had an apartment.

    a. have   **b.** will have   **c.** didn't have   **d.** hadn't

5. I .... very hungry yesterday.

    a. was   **b.** am   **c.** had   **d.** didn't have

2 Réécris ces phrases en utilisant **have got** à la forme qui convient. Dans quelle phrase est-ce impossible ? Pourquoi ?

1. My aunt has a small house and she doesn't have a car.

....

2. We didn't have much money, but we had a great time.

....

3. I have ten cousins, but I don't have any brothers or sisters.

....

4. I'm very happy. I have everything I want.

....

3 Complète avec le verbe **be**, au présent ou au prétérit. Utilise la forme contractée chaque fois que c'est possible.

1. Yesterday Lucy and I .... so sad. Today we .... so happy!

2. Yesterday you .... in London. Today you .... in Miami. .... (not) you tired?

3. Kevin, you .... (not) with your sister. But you .... with her this morning.

4. No, I .... (not) with her now and we .... (not) together this morning.

5. My friend Bob and his cousin Sasha .... thirteen years old. I .... one year younger.

6. Who .... your best friend now? And who .... your best friend last year?

2 | Décrire quelqu'un

@)) My mother is quite old, but she's **pretty**. Though I find her **tall** and **slim**, she thinks she's too **small** and too **fat,** and she often tries to lose weight and **look** younger.

Ma mère est assez âgée, mais elle est jolie. Bien que je la trouve grande et mince, elle pense qu'elle est trop petite et trop grosse, et elle essaie souvent de perdre du poids et d'avoir l'air plus jeune.

✳ Physical appearance (l'apparence physique)

- to look (+ adj.) : avoir l'air
- good-looking, 'beautiful : beau
- pretty /prɪti/ : joli
- 'ugly : laid
- tall, big : grand

- small, short : petit
- strong : fort
- fat : gros
- slim : mince

✳ The face and the body (le visage et le corps)

- the eye /aɪ/ : l'œil
- the chin /tʃɪn/ : le menton
- the mouth /maʊθ/ : la bouche
- the nose : le nez
- the ear /ɪə/ : l'oreille
- a tooth (pl. teeth) : une dent
- 'freckles : des taches de rousseur
- hair : les cheveux
- brown /aʊ/ : châtain
- dark : brun, foncé
- fair : blond, clair
- blond : blond
- red : roux

- the head /e/ : la tête
- the neck : le cou
- the arm : le bras
- the hand : la main
- a finger : un doigt
- the thumb /θʌm/ : le pouce
- the leg : la jambe
- the knee : le genou
- the foot (pl. feet) : le pied
- straight /streɪt/ : raide
- curly : bouclé
- short : court

✳ Clothes /kləʊðz/, shoes and accessories (vêtements, chaussures et accessoires)

- to wear*/eə/ : porter (un vêtement)
- a shirt /ɜː/ : une chemise
- trousers /aʊ/ (GB), pants (US) : un pantalon
- a sweater /swetə/, a jumper : un pull-over
- a skirt /ɜː/ : une jupe
- a dress : une robe
- a tracksuit : un survêtement
- a jacket : une veste
- a coat /əʊ/ : un manteau
- socks : des chaussettes

- tights /taɪts/ : un collant
- boots : des bottes
- trainers (GB), sneakers (US) : des baskets
- a cap : une casquette
- a scarf /ɑː/ (pl. scarves) : une écharpe, un foulard
- a belt : une ceinture
- a watch : une montre
- 'earrings : des boucles d'oreille

Exercices

1 Voici des élèves de ma classe. Lis chaque description et devine qui sont mes amis.

| Peter | Bryan | Shirley | Bob | Tina | Fiona |

1. She has got long hair. Her hair is straight but it looks nice. She is wearing a black jacket, a short skirt and beautiful earrings on the picture.

What is her name? ....

2. He is slim but he isn't very tall. He has got curly hair and big eyes. He is wearing a shirt.

Who is he? ....

3. He is quite tall and has got short dark hair. His mouth looks very big on the photo. He is wearing a Tee-shirt.

Can you guess his name? ....

4. She has got short hair and a small nose. She is wearing a tracksuit and trainers.

Who is she? ....

> ▪ nice : gentil

2 Raye l'intrus de chacune des listes.

1. good-looking – beautiful – strong – pretty

2. tall – slim – short – small

3. nose – eyes – legs – ears

4. hand – thumb – finger – head

5. a shirt – a sweater – a jumper – a watch

6. earrings – shoes – trainers – boots

7. socks – scarves – tights – shoes

8. blond – curly – red – fair

3 De quoi s'agit-il ? Écris le mot en anglais.

1. Ce sont de jolis petits points que l'on peut avoir sur le visage ou le corps : ....

2. Il se trouve sous la bouche : ....

3. C'est un doigt à part : ....

4. On les met avant d'enfiler ses chaussures : ....

5. On l'attache pour tenir son pantalon : ....

3 | Les deux présents

> On emploie surtout le présent simple pour parler d'une action régulière. Avec le présent en **be + -ing,** on parle d'une action en cours au moment où on parle.

✹ Le présent simple

● Il ne faut surtout pas oublier d'ajouter un **-S** à la 3ᵉ personne du singulier et il faut retenir que **do** /duː/ s'écrit **does** /dʌz/ à la 3ᵉ personne du singulier.

	I/we/you/they	he/she/it
affirmation	I **work** here. Je travaille ici.	Linh **workS** here. Linh travaille ici.
négation	I **don't work** here. I **do not work** here. Je ne travaille pas ici.	Linh **doESn't work** here. Linh **doES not work** here. Lihn ne travaille pas ici.
interrogation	**Do** you **work** here? Est-ce que tu travailles ici ?	**DoES** Linh **work** here? Est-ce que Linh travaille ici ?

● On emploie le présent simple pour parler d'une action régulière. On l'emploie donc avec des adverbes de fréquence comme **always** (toujours), **never** (jamais), **often** (souvent).
I **go** to school every day but **never** at the weekend!
Je vais à l'école tous les jours mais jamais le week-end !

✹ Le présent en be + -ing

● Pour conjuguer le présent en **be + -ing**, il faut conjuguer **be** au présent suivi du verbe **+ -ing**.

	I	he/she/it	we/ you/ they
affirmation	I**'m** writ**ing**. I **am** writ**ing**.	He**'s** writ**ing**. He **is** writ**ing**.	They**'re** writ**ing**. They **are** writ**ing**.
négation	I**'m not** writ**ing**. I **am not** writ**ing**.	He **isn't** writ**ing**. He **is not** writ**ing**.	They **aren't** writ**ing**. They **are not** writ**ing**.
interrogation	**Am** I writ**ing**?	**Is** he writ**ing**?	**Are** they writ**ing**?

● On emploie le présent en **be + -ing** pour dire qu'une action ou un fait est en cours au moment où on parle.
"What **are** you **doing**, Sam?" "I**'m writing** an essay."
« Qu'est-ce que tu fais, Sam ? – Je suis en train d'écrire une rédaction. »

◉ Certains verbes ne s'emploient presque jamais avec la forme en **be + -ing**.
Les principaux sont **agree** (être d'accord), **believe** (croire), **know** (savoir), **hate** (détester), **like** (bien aimer), **love** (aimer), **prefer** (préférer), **remember** (se souvenir), **seem** (sembler), **understand** (comprendre), **want** (vouloir).
I **know** you **understand** English.
Je sais que tu comprends l'anglais.

Exercices

1 **Mets les verbes entre parenthèses au présent simple. Attention aux formes interrogative et négative.**

1. .... (you/know) Mrs Harper?

2. .... (Mrs Harper/know) you?

3. Mrs Harper .... (want) to meet your dad.

4. She .... (not/want) to call him.

5. I .... (hope) that she .... (understand) him.
My dad .... (not/speak) English well!

2 **Mets les verbes entre parenthèses au présent en be + -ing. Utilise les formes contractées quand c'est possible.**

1. I .... (enjoy) this film. What about you?

2. We .... (learn) English and we .... (have) fun.

3. .... (your parents/go) to London this weekend?

4. No, they .... (not/go) to London, they .... (fly) to Ireland tomorrow.

5. Sue .... (not/watch) television right now. She .... (write) an essay.

3 **Transforme ces phrases affirmatives en phrases négatives et interrogatives.**

1. Chris works very hard. ....

2. Jo's cats eat a lot. ....

3. They're eating right now. ....

4. I'm talking too loud. ....

5. Kitty is fighting with Winky. ....

> **Coup de pouce**
> La phrase interrogative doit commencer par un auxiliaire (**be** ou **do**).
> Il faut aussi un auxiliaire dans la phrase négative (**be** ou **do**).

▪ too loud : trop fort

4 **Mets le verbe à la forme qui convient : présent simple ou présent en be + -ing.**

Lucy – "Mum, we shouldn't take the car. It .... (snow)!"

Mum – "What? But it never .... (snow) here! It .... (rain) a lot,
but it never .... (snow)!"

Lucy – "Look, Mum. What .... (be) that in the sky?"

Mum – "Oh look! Some people .... (make) a film. It .... (be) artificial
snow."

Lucy – "So, it .... (not/snow)? How sad."

Mum – "I .... (agree) with you. I .... (prefer) snow to rain.
But right now I .... (be) glad it .... (not/snow)."

4 Exprimer ses goûts, ses sentiments

@)) I **hate** doing the housework and I **can't stand** doing the washing-up, whereas my brother **doesn't mind.** So, it doesn't matter if he always does it... Does it?

Je déteste faire le ménage et je ne supporte pas de faire la vaisselle, alors que mon frère, lui, ça ne le dérange pas. Donc, ça ne fait rien si c'est lui qui la fait toujours... N'est-ce pas ?

✳ Likes and dislikes (ce que l'on aime et ce que l'on n'aime pas)

- to like : aimer
- to love : aimer, adorer
- to pre'fer, to like … better/best : préférer
- favourite /ˈfeɪvərɪt/ : préféré
- to be* crazy/mad about : être fou de
- to be* keen on : être emballé par
- to be* fond of : être amateur de

- to enjoy : prendre plaisir à
- to be* interested in : s'intéresser à
- to dislike : ne pas aimer
- to hate : détester
- I can't stand/bear /beə/ : je ne supporte pas
- I don't mind /aɪ/ : ça m'est égal
- I don't care /keə/ : je m'en fiche

✳ 'Happiness and sadness (le bonheur et la tristesse)

- 'happy : heureux
- 'merry : joyeux
- pleased /pliːzd/, glad /æ/ : content
- to smile /aɪ/ : sourire
- to laugh /lɑːf/ : rire
- ex'citing : passionnant, captivant
- sad : triste

- 'miserable : malheureux
- disap'pointed : déçu
- 'desperate /desprɪt/ : désespéré
- to cry, to weep* : pleurer
- to feel* bored : s'ennuyer
- boring, dull /ʌ/ : ennuyeux
- annoyed : contrarié

✳ Anger /ˈæŋɡə/, fear /fɪə/ and sur'prise (la colère, la peur et la surprise)

- to be 'angry with sb : être en colère contre qqn
- to lose* one's temper : se mettre en colère
- furious /ˈfjuərɪəs/ : très en colère
- cross (with) : fâché (contre)
- fright /fraɪt/ : la peur, l'effroi
- frightening : effrayant

- frightened /ˈfraɪtənd/, scared : effrayé
- to frighten /aɪ/, to scare /skeə/ : effrayer, faire peur à
- to be afraid of : avoir peur de
- sur'prised /aɪ/ : surpris
- sur'prising /aɪ/ : surprenant
- unex'pected : inattendu
- unbe'lievable : incroyable

✳ Hopes and regrets (les espoirs et les regrets)

- to hope : espérer
- 'hopeful : plein d'espoir
- to wish : souhaiter

- to ex'pect : s'attendre à, compter sur
- to be 'sorry : être désolé
- to re'gret : regretter

1 Trouve l'adjectif commençant par la lettre proposée pour décrire les personnages ci-dessous.

1. H..   **3.** F..   **5.** S..

2. S..   **4.** B..   **6.** A..

2 Remets ces lettres dans l'ordre pour trouver le mot qui correspond à chaque définition.

1. Quand on n'aime pas : KIEDSIL ....

2. On nage dedans quand on est heureux : IPSHSAPNE ....

3. L'école l'est parfois, mais jamais les cours d'anglais (!) : NGOBIR ....

4. Quand on croit en l'avenir : PUHFLOE ....

5. Une surprise l'est toujours : GSSPURIRNI ....

3 Lis ce mail de Sebastian, ton correspondant anglais.

Hi there!
Thank you for your message. It seems that we have a lot in common, which is great!
I do lots of sport too: I love swimming and I'm very keen on judo. But I don't really like playing tennis.
At school, my favourite subject is Science because I like my Science teacher very much, and I'm also very interested in languages, especially French. But I hate Geography... I think it's boring! Which subjects do <u>you</u> like?
Tell me asap.

Sebastian

■ asap : as soon as possible

Récapitule les goûts de Sebastian en classant les mots suivants dans la bonne colonne :
natation, judo, tennis, langues (français), géographie.

	♥	♥
sports		
matières scolaires		

5 | Les deux prétérits

En anglais, il existe deux prétérits :
– le prétérit simple pour dire ce qui s'est produit dans le passé ;
– le prétérit en **be + -ing** pour parler d'une action en cours à un moment du passé.

✳ Le prétérit simple

● Le prétérit simple se forme en ajoutant **-ed** aux <u>verbes réguliers</u>. On emploie la même forme à toutes les personnes.

	I/he/she/it/we/you/they
affirmation	I **worked** hard. J'ai travaillé dur.
négation	You **didn't** (**did not**) **work** hard. Tu n'as pas travaillé dur.
interrogation	**Did** they **work** hard? Est-ce qu'ils ont travaillé dur ?

Quelques verbes sont <u>irréguliers</u> (voir p. 54) :

eat (infinitif) → ate (prétérit)   run (infinitif) → ran (prétérit)
see (infinitif) → saw (prétérit)   understand (infinitif) → understood (prétérit)

● À la forme négative, on emploie « **didn't** + verbe » à toutes les personnes. Donc la formation est <u>la même</u> pour les verbes réguliers et les verbes irréguliers.
I **didn't** call.   They **didn't** understand.
Je n'ai pas appelé.   Ils n'ont pas compris.

● Dans une question, on a l'ordre « **did** + sujet + verbe ».
Did she call?   **Did** they understand?
Est-ce qu'elle a appelé?   Est-ce qu'ils ont compris?

● Le prétérit simple est la forme la plus employée pour parler du passé. On l'utilise en particulier quand on raconte une histoire ou quand on parle d'un passé coupé du présent.
I **made** a cake yesterday.
J'ai fait un gâteau hier.

✴ Le prétérit en be + -ing

● Le prétérit en **be + -ing** se forme avec **be** au prétérit (voir p. 6) suivi du verbe + **-ing**.
I **was** writ**ing**.   **Were** you eat**ing**?
J'étais en train d'écrire.   Est-ce que tu étais en train de manger?
She **wasn't** runn**ing**.
Elle n'était pas en train de courir.

● On emploie le prétérit en **be + -ing** pour dire qu'une action était <u>en cours</u> à un moment du passé. Le prétérit en **be + -ing** se traduit par l'imparfait.
"Who **were** you **talking** to?" "I **was chatting** with a classmate."
« À qui parlais-tu ? – Je bavardais avec un copain de classe. »

Exercices

1 Tim envoie un message à Sue en lui racontant ce qu'il a fait hier.
Réécris ce message en commençant par **Yesterday...**

I wake up early. It's 6 o'clock and I'm already late. I have to catch a train at 7:00.
I first have a shower and then I eat breakfast. I run out of the house. I catch a bus.
But when I arrive at the station at 7:10 I see that the train is twenty minutes late...

Yesterday I woke up early...

....

....

....

2 Transforme ces phrases affirmatives en questions.
Mrs Baker went to London. Did Mrs Baker go to London?

Coup de pouce

Pense à commencer les questions par un auxiliaire.

1. The Simpsons were watching TV at 7 o'clock.

....

2. It was raining hard.

....

3. She called Kris at lunch time.

....

4. They were complaining about the noise.

....

3 Complète ces phrases avec les groupes de mots proposés.

1. We .... to London when you called us.

2. I .... you because it was midnight.

3. I saw Leslie this morning. She .... breakfast with Paul.

4. Jim .... the New York marathon last year.

5. Do you think he .... himself?

6. It .... so hard you couldn't see anything.

- didn't call
- ran
- were driving
- was having
- was raining
- enjoyed

4 Complète en utilisant le même verbe (au prétérit) que dans la phrase de départ.

1. I **didn't know** you were Laura's brother! But I .... she had a brother.

2. They **didn't stand up** when you came in. They .... up when Mrs Kim came in.

3. Sandra **didn't cut** the bread for you. She .... it for me!

4. They **didn't steal** fifty dollars. They .... fifty cents.

5. I **didn't buy** any meat. I just .... some vegetables.

Coup de pouce Attention aux verbes irréguliers (voir p. 54).

1 Écoute et répète ces phrases en faisant particulièrement attention à la prononciation du verbe **be**, qui est en gras. Coche la case lorsque le verbe doit se prononcer dans sa forme pleine.

> **Rappel**
> **am** /əm/ (forme inaccentuée) mais /æm/ en fin de phrase (forme pleine)
> **are** /ə/ (forme inaccentuée) mais /ɑː/ en fin de phrase (forme pleine)
> **was** /wəz/ (forme inaccentuée) mais /wɒz/ en fin de phrase (forme pleine)
> **were** /wə/ (forme inaccentuée) mais /wɜː/ en fin de phrase (forme pleine)
> **is** /z/ (forme inaccentuée) mais /ɪz/ en fin de phrase (forme pleine)

1. "**Are** you sure he **is** there?" "Yes, I **am**."   ☐ Are   ☐ is   ☐ am

2. He **was** not present but Liz **was**.   ☐ was   ☐ was

3. "**Is** she your sister?" "No, she **is** my niece!"   ☐ Is   ☐ is

4. "**Are** they ready to go?" "Oh! Yes, they **are**!"   ☐ Are   ☐ are

5. I **am** sure he **is** at school.   ☐ am   ☐ is

6. "Who **is** this girl? She **is** pretty!" "She **is**, indeed!"   ☐ is   ☐ is   ☐ is

2 Écoute le document suivant puis complète les informations demandées.

1. Name of the person interviewed: ....

2. The music he listened to when he was very young: ....

3. The music he listened to when he was a teenager: ....

4. The sort of music he is making now: ☐ classical   ☐ pop   ☐ R'n'B   ☐ rock

5. His favourite instrument: ....

3 Écoute et répète les mots suivants en soulignant à chaque fois la syllabe accentuée (prononcée « plus » que les autres).

communication – action – conversation – protection – information – suggestion – imagination – participation – inspiration – convention

Où est située à chaque fois la syllabe accentuée dans un mot qui finit en -tion ?

....

Le nom en **-tion** est formé à partir d'un verbe. Retrouve à l'aide des mots précédents les verbes signifiant :

1. communiquer : ....
2. converser : ....
3. imaginer : ....
4. agir : ....
5. protéger : ....
6. suggérer : ....

4 Classe ces verbes selon la prononciation de la terminaison **-ed** du prétérit.
turned – picked – sounded – typed – walked – played – practiced – wanted – opened – closed – decided – liked

/d/	/t/	/ɪd/

5 Les mots français suivants sont prononcés « à l'anglaise » par des touristes étrangers qui demandent leur chemin. Les reconnais-tu ?

1. ....
2. ....
3. ....
4. ....
5. ....
6. ....

6 Comment prononcer la lettre soulignée dans les mots suivants ? Complète le tableau et vérifie à l'écoute.
plea<u>s</u>ure – <u>S</u>ean – plea<u>s</u>e – <u>s</u>alt – <u>s</u>ure! – <u>s</u>pecies – spe<u>c</u>ies – na<u>t</u>ion – trea<u>s</u>ure – no<u>s</u>e – pre<u>c</u>ious – mea<u>s</u>ure

paSS /s/	SHine /ʃ/	garaGe /ʒ/	daiSy /z/

7 Les mots suivants comportent tous au moins une lettre muette. Écoute, et barre les lettres que tu n'entends pas.

PRECIOUS   HOLMES   CASTLE   LISTEN   KNEE   ANSWER

KNOW   HALF   KNOWLEDGE   CUPBOARD   WHOLE   PLUMBER

8 Écoute les paires de mots suivantes et coche celles dont les deux mots ont la même prononciation.

- [ ] hair – hare
- [ ] where – here
- [ ] whole – hole
- [ ] find – fiend
- [ ] sow – saw
- [ ] pair – pear
- [ ] pear – peer
- [ ] right – write
- [ ] reed – read
- [ ] read – ride

7 ## Les modaux

> Les modaux (ou auxiliaires modaux) sont des verbes un peu particuliers.
> – Ils ne prennent <u>pas de **s** à la 3e personne du singulier</u>.
> – Ils sont suivis directement de **not** à la forme négative.
> – Ils ne sont jamais suivis de **to**.

✳ Can + verbe

● Avec **can**, on dit que quelqu'un <u>sait faire</u> ou <u>peut faire</u> quelque chose.

You **can** carry your suitcase.
Tu peux porter ta valise.

Can you use a computer?
Est-ce que tu sais utiliser un ordinateur ?

● Avec **can**, on peut aussi parler de <u>permission</u>.

You **can** have an ice cream if you eat your vegetables first.
Tu peux avoir une glace si tu manges d'abord tes légumes.

● Dans les <u>négations</u>, on emploie la forme contractée **can't**.

You **can't** carry it. [incapacité]
Tu ne peux pas la porter.

You **can't** stay here. [interdiction]
Vous ne pouvez pas rester ici.

● Dans les <u>questions</u>, l'ordre est « **can** + sujet ».

Can you carry it?
Est-ce que tu peux la porter ?

Can we stay here?
Est-ce qu'on peut rester ici ?

✳ May + verbe

● Avec **may**, on dit que quelque chose se fera <u>peut-être</u>.

They **may** go to Washington.
Ils iront peut-être à Washington.

They **may** not go to Washington. [probabilité négative]
Ils n'iront peut-être pas à Washington.

● On peut aussi utiliser **may** pour demander une <u>permission</u>.

May I borrow your phone?
Est-ce que je peux emprunter votre téléphone ?

You **may** not use this computer. [interdiction]
Vous n'avez pas le droit d'utiliser cet ordinateur.

✳ Must + verbe

● Avec **must**, on dit que quelqu'un <u>doit faire</u> quelque chose.

You **must** say hello to your grandma.
Tu dois dire bonjour à ta grand-mère.

● Dans les <u>négations</u>, on emploie **must not** ou la forme contractée **mustn't**.

You **mustn't** say that. [interdiction]
Tu ne dois pas dire ça.

✳ Should + verbe

Avec **should**, on exprime un conseil (tu devrais, vous devriez...).

You **should** call a doctor.
Tu devrais appeler un médecin.

Exercices

1 Choisis le sens de ces modaux : capacité, permission, obligation ou conseil.

1. This car can do 200 kilometers an hour. ....

2. Dad just called. We must wait for him here. ....

3. Mum said we can watch TV. ....

4. The teacher says we may enter now. ....

5. Kevin, you should keep Fifi on a lead. ....

6. You must do your homework now. ....

> ■ a lead : une laisse

2 Complète à l'aide d'un modal en t'aidant des indications entre crochets.

1. You're tired. You .... rest a bit. [conseil]

2. Of course, you .... run faster. Make an effort! [capacité]

3. I .... go to your party. I have a fever! [incapacité]

4. Everybody .... sing, but not everyone .... sing in tune. [capacité]

5. Honey, you .... wash your hands before dinner. [obligation]

6. Mummy, ... I watch TV? [permission]

7. No, you .... watch TV. It's too late. [interdiction]

> ■ to sing in tune : chanter juste   ■ to rest : se reposer

3 Traduis en utilisant des modaux.

« Maman, est-ce que Rex peut avoir une glace ?
– Non, un chien ne devrait pas manger de glace.
– Est-ce qu'il a le droit de manger un os ?
– Oui, mais il doit manger dehors. Il ne doit pas rester ici.
– Pauvre Rex, tu peux faire ceci, tu ne peux pas faire cela.
Ce n'est pas une vie. »

....

....

....

....

....

> ■ Ce n'est pas une vie. That's no life.

8 | Saluer, se présenter, inviter

@)) Hello, **my name is** Mrs Johnson, I'm your English teacher, and **this is** Jane, our English assistant. I'd also like you to meet Deborah, a new pupil.

Bonjour, je m'appelle Mme Johnson, je suis votre professeur d'anglais, et voici Jane, notre assistante d'anglais. J'aimerais aussi vous présenter Déborah, une nouvelle élève.

✳ Greetings and introductions (les salutations et les présentations)

- Hello! /həˈləʊ/ Bonjour !
- Hi! /ˈhaɪ/ Salut ! Bonjour !
- Good 'morning! Bonjour ! [avant midi]
- Good after'noon! Bonjour ! [après midi]
- Good 'evening! Bonsoir !
- Good night! Bonne nuit !
- Nice/glad/pleased /pliːzd/ to meet you! Ravi de vous/te rencontrer !
- 'Welcome (to)... Bienvenue (à/en)...

- Good'bye! Bye! Au revoir !
- See you soon! À bientôt !
- See you on Monday/on Tuesday... À lundi/ À mardi...
- My name is..., I am... Je m'appelle...
- This is..., Here is... Voici...
- to meet* : rencontrer, faire la connaissance de
- to introduce /ɪntrəˈdjuːs/ : présenter

✳ Polite words and wishes (les politesses et les souhaits)

- Please /iː/... S'il vous plaît.../S'il te plaît...
- Excuse me... Pardon... Excuse(z)-moi...
- Pardon /ˈpɑːdn/? Pardon ?
- How are you? Comment ça va ?
- Very well, thank you. Très bien, merci.
- Thank /θæŋk/ you very much! Thanks a lot! Merci beaucoup.
- You're 'welcome! De rien !

- (God) bless you! À tes souhaits ! [quand on éternue]
- Congratulations /kəngrætjʊˈleɪʃnz/! Félicitations !
- Get well soon... Bon rétablissement !
- Good luck! Bonne chance !
- Have a nice day! Bonne journée !

✳ Invitations /ɪnvɪˈteɪʃnz/ (les invitations)

- to in'vite /aɪ/ : inviter
- a friend /frend/ : un ami
- to come* over for dinner/lunch/tea : venir dîner/déjeuner/goûter
- to come* in : entrer
- to sit* down, to have* a seat : s'asseoir
- to bring* /brɪŋ/ sth : apporter qqch.
- Would you like to (+ V)? Voudrais-tu/Voudriez-vous (+ V) ?
- Sure /ʃɔː/! Bien sûr !

- All right! OK! D'accord !
- Great! /eɪ/ Super !
- I'd love to : j'aimerais beaucoup
- to be* sorry : être désolé, regretter
- to be* busy /ˈbɪzi/ : être occupé
- to 'celebrate : fêter, faire la fête
- a 'party : une fête
- an anni'versary : un anniversaire [événement]
- a birthday /ˈbɜːθdeɪ/ : un anniversaire [personne]

Exercices

1 Que peux-tu répondre à ton interlocuteur dans les situations suivantes ? Coche la réponse qui convient.

1. Good morning !
☐ Good evening!
☐ Hello!
☐ Goodbye!
☐ Good luck!

2. Nice to meet you.
☐ I'd like to meet you.
☐ You're welcome!
☐ Pleased to meet you!
☐ Get well soon.

3. How are you?
☐ Fine, thank you.
☐ Nice to meet you.
☐ You're welcome!
☐ Thank you very much.

4. Thanks a lot.
☐ I'd love to.
☐ Welcome to my place...
☐ Bless you!
☐ You're welcome!

5. Would you like to go to the cinema tonight?
☐ I'd love to.
☐ See you soon!
☐ Congratulations!
☐ Nice to meet you.

2 Pour ses douze ans, Sebby organise une fête sur le thème des pirates dans son jardin, le samedi 14 avril à 15 h 00. Complète l'invitation qu'il adresse à Lora.

INVITATION

Dear ....

You're invited to

my .... party!

Place: 5, Mill street,

in the ....

Date:

....

Time:

....

Dress code: dress up as

....

From: ....

▪ to dress up : se déguiser

3 Lora et Alex ont répondu à l'invitation par téléphone. Mais Sebby ne comprend pas bien les messages qu'ils ont laissés. Aide-le à les reconstituer en entourant la meilleure proposition parmi les mots colorés.

1. Hi/Bye/Pardon, Sebby. This is/My name is/I'm Lora. Thanks/ Thank/Nice you very much for your invitation. I'd be very happy to come to your party. Welcome/See you/Bye on Saturday!

2. It's me Alex. I'm very busy/happy/sorry I can't come to your anniversary/party/invitation. I'm busy/happy/sorry on Saturday: I'm babysitting my little brother. But I wish you a very happy evening/birthday/day.

9

L'expression de l'avenir

Voici deux façons de parler de l'avenir : avec **will** et avec **be going to**. Avec **will**, on dit que quelque chose arrivera. Avec **be going to,** on prédit quelque chose ou on parle d'une décision déjà prise.

✳ Will + verbe

● Avec **will,** on se projette dans l'avenir et on dit qu'on est sûr que quelque chose se fera.
Sam **will** be 13 next year.
Sam aura 13 ans l'année prochaine. (C'est sûr !)
I**'ll** send you a postcard!
Je t'enverrai une carte postale ! (Je le garantis.)

● **Will** est très facile à conjuguer : on l'utilise à toutes les personnes !
I will be / you will be / he will be…
Je serai / tu seras / il sera…

● Après un pronom, **will** est souvent contracté en **'ll.**
I**'ll** be / you**'ll** be / he**'ll** be / she**'ll** be / it**'ll** be / we**'ll** be / they**'ll** be

● À la forme négative, on ajoute **not** après le modal.
I **will not** send them a postcard!
Je ne leur enverrai pas de carte postale !

● **Will not** est souvent contracté en **won't** /wəʊnt/.
I **won't** send them a postcard!

○ **Will** est un modal. Il ne prend donc pas de **-s** à la 3e personne du singulier.
Sam **will** be 13 next year.

✳ Be going to + verbe

● On utilise **be going to** pour <u>prédire</u> quelque chose à partir d'un indice présent.
Look! It**'s going to** rain.
Regarde ! Il va pleuvoir. [Indice : de gros nuages.]
Careful, Jo! You**'re going to** fall.
Attention, Jo ! Tu vas tomber. [Indice possible : Jo court trop vite.]

● On peut aussi employer **be going to** pour parler d'une <u>décision</u> déjà prise.
We**'re going to** visit Scotland during the holidays.
On va visiter l'Écosse pendant les vacances.

● Pour conjuguer **be going to,** il suffit de savoir conjuguer le verbe **be** (voir p. 6).
I'm going to visit… / you're going to visit… / she's going to visit…

Exercices

1 **Will ou be going to ?** Mets le verbe à la forme qui convient dans ces phrases qui renvoient à l'avenir. Utilise les formes contractées chaque fois que c'est possible.

1. My little brother .... (be) eight years old next month.

2. I .... (see) you tomorrow, Luke!

3. It's cold and grey. It .... (snow).

4. The train leaves in five minutes, so we .... (arrive) in London in two hours.

5. Harrison .... (not / come) with us if he's still sick.

6. My mum is fed up with her old car. She .... (get) a new car soon.

> ■ to be fed up with : en avoir assez de

Dans quelles phrases as-tu employé **be going to**? .... Pourquoi ? ....

2 Complète ces phrases avec **be going to.** Utilise les formes contractées chaque fois que c'est possible.

1. I .... (not) lie to you: you failed.

2. We .... take the first train to Cambridge.

3. Don't worry, it .... (not) rain.

4. You .... (not) pass if you don't work a bit harder.

5. She .... have an accident if she drives so fast.

6. You .... regret it, so tell her how you feel.

3 Transforme ces affirmations en questions.

1. Kelly will be with her parents. ....

2. It's going to take a long time. ....

3. We're going to listen to Mike's presentation. ....

4. They're going to play basketball. ....

5. I'm going to be late. ....

6. It will be dark when we get there. ....

4 Dis à Jessica en anglais :

1. Je vais repeindre ma chambre. ....

2. Je serai vétérinaire un jour. ....

3. Je ne jouerai pas au rugby l'année prochaine. ....

4. Il va pleuvoir. N'oublie pas ton parapluie! ....

5. J'arriverai à midi s'il ne neige pas. ....

> ■ repeindre : to redecorate   ■ un vétérinaire : a vet   ■ midi : noon

10 À la maison

@)) A typical Victorian **house**, built during Queen Victoria's reign, usually has a **porch**, a **bay window**, a **basement** with a **cellar** to store coal, and **sash windows**.

Une maison victorienne typique, construite pendant le règne de la reine Victoria, comprend généralement un porche, une fenêtre en saillie, un sous-sol avec une cave pour stocker le charbon et des fenêtres à guillotine.

✳ An English house (une maison anglaise)

- a fence : une clôture
- a porch : un porche
- a door : une porte
- a window : une fenêtre
- a bay window : une fenêtre en saillie
- a sash window : une fenêtre à guillotine
- the roof : le toit
- the attic : le grenier

- a chimney : une cheminée [conduit]
- the floor /ɔː/, the ground : le sol
- a step : une marche
- the cellar : la cave
- the basement : le sous-sol
- the garage /ˈgærɑːʒ/ : le garage
- the garden : le jardin
- the lawn /ɔː/ : la pelouse

✳ Living room and dining room (séjour et salle à manger)

- furniture /ˈfɜːnɪtʃə/ : les meubles
- a curtain /ˈkɜːtn/ : un rideau
- a carpet : un tapis
- a fireplace : une cheminée
- the settee, the sofa : le canapé
- a chair : une chaise

- the cupboard /ˈkʌbəd/ : l'armoire, le placard
- the sideboard : le buffet
- a bulb : une ampoule
- the television set : la télévision
- a remote control : une télécommande

✳ The bedroom (la chambre)

- a bed : un lit
- a bedside table : une table de chevet
- a bookcase : une bibliothèque
- a wardrobe : une armoire
- a chest of drawers : une commode

- a drawer : un tiroir
- a desk : un bureau
- a shelf (pl. : shelves) : une étagère
- a mirror : un miroir

✳ The bathroom (la salle de bains)

- the basin /ˈbeɪsn/ : le lavabo
- the shower /ˈʃaʊə/ : la douche
- a bath : un bain, une baignoire
- soap : du savon
- shampoo : du shampooing

- a towel /ˈtaʊəl/ : une serviette
- a toothbrush : une brosse à dents
- toothpaste : du dentifrice
- a comb /kəʊm/ : un peigne
- a brush : une brosse

Exercices

1 À partir de ce dessin, trouve les noms anglais correspondant aux numéros.

1. ....
2. ....
3. ....
4. ....
5. ....
6. ....
7. ....
8. ....

2 Nomme les éléments représentés puis attribue chacun à la pièce où on le trouve.

1. ....
2. ....
3. ....
4. ....
5. ....
6. ....

In the study: ....   the living room: ....   the bedroom: ....   the bathroom: ....

3 Entoure les éléments que l'on peut trouver à l'intérieur d'une maison.

a bulb – a remote control – a chimney – a porch – a piece of furniture – a desk –

the lawn – a fence – a fireplace – a shower

4 Traduis les mots suivants et forme à partir des lettres en couleur le mot qui correspond à cette définition : il relie les pièces.

1. tapis : ▭ __ __ __ __ __

2. miroir : __ __ __ __ ▭ __

3. armoire : __ __ ▭ __ __ __ __

4. brosse : __ ▭ __ __ __

5. grenier : __ __ __ ▭ __

6. table de chevet : __ __ __ __ __ __ ▭ __   __ __ __ __ __

7. bibliothèque : __ __ ▭ __ __ __ __

8. cave : __ __ __ __ ▭ __

Mot mystère : __ __ __ __ __ __ __

11 Les pronoms personnels

Les pronoms personnels servent à désigner des personnes, des animaux ou des objets. Il ne faut pas confondre pronoms sujets et pronoms compléments.

pronoms personnels sujets	pronoms personnels compléments
I	me
you	you
he/she/it	him/her/it
we	us
you	you
they	them

✴ Les pronoms personnels sujets

● On emploie les pronoms personnels sujets comme en français.

I know Josh.
Je connais Josh.

We know your parents.
Nous connaissons tes parents.

(👁 **I** (1re personne du singulier) s'écrit toujours avec une majuscule !

● À la 3e personne du singulier, on emploie **it** pour une chose ou un animal, sauf si c'est un animal familier (**he** ou **she**).

Where is Beauty? She's not in her kennel.
Où est Beauty ? Elle n'est pas dans sa niche.

● **It** s'emploie aussi pour parler du temps qu'il fait ou pour donner l'heure.

It's raining.
Il pleut.

It's snowing.
Il neige.

It's sunny.
Il fait beau.

It's five o'clock.
Il est cinq heures.

● L'équivalent de « moi, je… » est simplement **I**, accentué à l'oral. À l'écrit, on souligne **I** pour signaler qu'il est accentué.

I don't like it.
Moi, je n'aime pas ça.

✴ Les pronoms personnels compléments

● Les pronoms personnels compléments n'ont qu'une seule forme : **me, you, him, her, it, us, them**. En français, on a parfois deux formes : « me/moi », « te/toi »…

● En anglais, les pronoms personnels compléments se placent toujours <u>après</u> le verbe. En français, ils se placent parfois avant le verbe.

I'm talking about **her**.
Je parle d'**elle**.

I can see **her**.
Je **la** vois.

Exercices

1 **Complète ces légendes avec un pronom personnel.**

1. .... is red.   **2.** .... is red.   **3.** .... is in red.

2 **Remplace les mots soulignés par un pronom personnel.**

1. My dog is called Rex. I love <u>Rex</u>.

....

2. Your parents are so nice. Can I say hello to <u>your parents</u>?

....

3. The train is here. I think we can now get on <u>the train</u>.

....

4. "I love Lucy". "Who is <u>Lucy</u>?"

....

5. The door is very heavy. I can't shut <u>the door</u>!

....

6. The bird is singing. Can you hear <u>the bird</u>?

....

3 **Complète ces phrases avec le pronom personnel qui convient. Aide-toi des mots soulignés.**

1. My <u>granddad</u> is coming tonight. .... is coming with my uncle.

2. My <u>aunt</u> is sick. .... can't come tonight.

3. This <u>computer</u> is new. I bought .... last month.

4. <u>My neighbours' cars</u> are old. .... want to sell ....

5. <u>Elizabeth</u> is my cousin. Do you want to meet ....? .... is very nice.

6. Oh, ... is late. Wake up, Mike! .... is 7 o'clock.

7. <u>Jack and I</u> are cousins, so .... have the same grandparents.

They give .... a lot of presents.

8. Don't use this <u>towel</u>. I want to wash ....

9. I can't find my <u>bag</u>. Do you know where .... is?

> ▪ a towel : une serviette

12 Sounds, sounds, sounds... @))

1 Écoute le document audio suivant et complète les informations demandées.

1. Name of the radio station: ....
Nom de la radio

2. Name of the guest: ....
Nom de l'invité

3. His job: ....
Son travail

Complète ce résumé de la discussion avec les mots qui conviennent.

The guest is going to accompany .... (identity)

to .... (country/continent) and will go to

.... (continent) in .... (date).

Que pense l'invité de ce voyage ? Coche la case qui convient.

☐ It's an opportunity.

☐ He doesn't want to go.

☐ It's great.

☐ It is not different from what he usually does.

▪ usually : habituellement

2 Écoute le document suivant et entoure la maison où habite Tom.

3 Écoute les mots suivants et souligne la syllabe accentuée.

inhabited	comfortable	tidy	attractive
patient	formal	friendly	polite

Corrigés
des exercices

1 — Les verbes *be* et *have* (p. 6)

1
1. Who **is** cold?
2. Who **has got** cousins in Edinburgh?
3. We **don't have** enough time.
4. We **didn't have** a house in New York, we had an apartment.
5. I **was** very hungry yesterday.

2
1. My aunt has got… she hasn't got…
2. Impossible dans cette phrase. Au prétérit on emploie **had** ou **didn't have** car have got n'existe qu'au présent.
3. I've got… I haven't got…
4. I've got everything…

3
1. Yesterday Lucy and I **were** so sad. Today we**'re** so happy!
2. Yesterday you **were** in London. Today you**'re** in Miami. **Aren't** you tired?
3. Kevin, you **aren't** ou **'re not** with your sister. But you **were** with her this morning.
4. No, I**'m not** with her now and we **weren't** together this morning.
5. My friend Bob and his cousin Sasha **are** thirteen years old. I**'m** one year younger.
6. Who**'s** your best friend now? And who **was** your best friend last year?

2 — Décrire quelqu'un (p. 8)

1
1. Shirley
2. Bob
3. Bryan
4. Tina

2
1. strong
2. slim (les autres adjectifs concernent la taille)
3. legs
4. head
5. a watch
6. earrings
7. scarves (tout le reste se met sur les pieds)
8. curly (les autres adjectifs indiquent la couleur des cheveux)

3
1. freckles
2. chin
3. thumb
4. socks
5. belt

3 — Les deux présents (p. 10)

1
1. **Do** you **know** Mrs Harper?
2. **Does** Mrs Harper **know** you?
3. Mrs Harper **wants** to meet your dad.
4. She **doesn't want** to call him.
5. I **hope** that she **understands** him. My dad **doesn't speak** English well!

2
1. I**'m enjoying** this film. What about you?
2. We**'re learning** English and we**'re having** fun.
3. **Are** your parents **going** to London this weekend?
4. No, they **aren't going** to London, they**'re flying** to Ireland tomorrow.
5. Sue **isn't watching** television right now. She**'s writing** an essay.

3
1. Chris doesn't work very hard. / Does Chris work very hard?
2. Jo's cats don't eat a lot. / Do Jo's cats eat a lot?
3. They aren't ou They're not eating right now. / Are they eating right now?
4. I'm not talking too loud. / Am I talking too loud?
5. Kitty isn't fighting with Winky. / Is Kitty fighting with Winky?

4
Lucy – "Mum, we shouldn't take the car. It**'s snowing**!"
Mum – "What? But it never **snows** here! It **rains** a lot, but it never **snows**!"
Lucy – "Look, Mum. What **is** that in the sky?"
Mum – "Oh, look, some people **are making** a film. It's artificial snow."
Lucy – "So, it **isn't snowing**? How sad."
Mum – "I **agree** with you. I **prefer** snow to rain. But right now I **am** glad it**'s** not (ou **isn't**) **snowing**."

4 — Exprimer ses goûts, ses sentiments (p. 12)

1
1. Happy
2. Sad
3. Frightened
4. Bored
5. Surprised
6. Angry

2
1. DISLIKE
2. HAPPINESS
3. BORING
4. HOPEFUL
5. SURPRISING

3

	♥	♥
sports	natation, judo	tennis
matières scolaires	sciences, langues (français)	géographie

5 — Les deux prétérits (p. 14)

1 Yesterday, I **woke up** early. It **was** 6 o'clock and I **was** already late. I **had** to catch a train at 7:00. I first **had** a shower and then I **ate** breakfast. I **ran** out of the house. I **caught** a bus. But when I **arrived** at the station at 7:10 I **saw** that the train **was** twenty minutes late…

2
1. Were the Simpsons watching TV at 7 o'clock?
2. Was it raining hard?
3. Did she call Kris at lunch time?
4. Were they complaining about the noise?

3
1. We **were driving** to London when you called us.
2. I **didn't call** you because it was midnight.
3. I saw Leslie this morning. She **was having** breakfast with Paul.
4. Jim **ran** the New York marathon last year.
5. Do you think he **enjoyed** himself?
6. It **was raining** so hard you couldn't see anything.

4
1. But I **knew** she had a brother.
2. They **stood** up when Mrs Kim came in.
3. She **cut** it for me!
4. They **stole** fifty cents.
5. I just **bought** some vegetables.

6 Sounds, sounds, sounds... @)) (p. 16)

1
1. "**Are** you sure he **is** there?" "Yes, I **am** ☑."
2. He **was** not present but Liz **was** ☑.
3. "**Is** she your sister?" "No, she **is** my niece!"
4. "**Are** they ready to go?" "Oh! Yes, they **are** ☑!"
5. I **am** sure he **is** at school.
6. "Who **is** this girl? She **is** pretty!" "She **is** ☑, indeed!"

Indeed, adverbe, n'a pas d'influence sur la prononciation de la réponse courte.

2
JACK – "Today, we are happy to host – not just a singer, but probably one of the best singers of the twenty-first century: Tom Peterson! Welcome, Tom."
TOM – "Thanks for inviting me, Jack."
JACK – "So, Tom. Who is your source of inspiration?"
TOM – "Well... When I was young, I liked the Beatles, and the Doors, the kind of music my parents listened to. But when I grew up and became a teenager, I preferred Oasis or James Blunt. That's when I decided to make pop music, really."
JACK – "What's your favourite instrument?"
TOM – "My... I'd say... the guitar, probably. Although I love playing the piano too. But the guitar corresponds more to the kind of music I make."

1. Name of the person interviewed: **Tom Peterson**
2. The music he listened to when he was very young: **the Beatles, the Doors**
3. The music he listened to when he was a teenager: **Oasis, James Blunt**
4. The sort of music he is making now: **pop**
5. His favourite instrument: **the guitar**

3 communication – action – conversation – protection – information – suggestion – imagination – participation – inspiration – convention

La syllabe accentuée est l'avant-dernière, celle située juste avant le suffixe **-tion**.

---

1. communiquer : commu**ni**cate
2. converser : con**ver**se
3. imaginer : i**ma**gine
4. agir : **act**
5. protéger : pro**tect**
6. suggérer : su**ggest**

L'ajout du suffixe déplace l'accent de mot : i**ma**gine → imagi**na**tion.

4

/d/	/t/	/ɪd/
turned, played, opened, closed	picked, typed, walked, practiced, liked	sounded, wanted, decided

5
1. Versailles
2. the Eiffel Tower (la tour Eiffel)
3. the Sacré Cœur
4. Grenoble
5. the Mont Saint-Michel
6. the musée d'Orsay

6

/s/	/ʃ/	/ʒ/	/z/
salt species	Sean sure! species nation precious	pleasure treasure measure	please nose

7 PRE**C**IOUS • HO**L**MES • CAS**T**LE • LIS**T**EN • **K**NEE • AN**S**WER • **K**NOW • HAL**F** • **K**NOWLEDGE • CUPBOAR**D** • **W**HOLE • PLUM**B**ER

8
☑ hair – hare   ☑ pair – pear
☐ where – here   ☐ pear – peer
☑ whole – hole   ☑ right – write
☐ find – fiend   ☑ reed – read
☐ sow – saw   ☐ read – ride

7 Les modaux (p. 18)

1
1. capacité
2. obligation
3. permission
4. permission
5. conseil
6. obligation

2
1. You're tired. You **should** rest a bit.
2. Of course, you **can** run faster. Make an effort!
3. I **can't** go to your party. I have a fever!
4. Everybody **can** sing, but not everyone **can** sing in tune.
5. Honey, you **must** wash your hands before dinner.
6. Mummy, **can** ou **may** I watch TV?
7. No, you **can't** ou **may not** watch TV. It's too late.

3 "Mum, can Rex have an ice cream?"
"No, a dog shouldn't eat ice cream."
"May ou Can he eat a bone?"

"Yes, he may ou can, but he must eat it outside.
He mustn't stay here."
"Poor Rex, you can do this, you can't do that.
That's no life."

8 Saluer, se présenter, inviter (p. 20)

1
1. Hello!
2. Pleased to meet you!
3. Fine, thank you.
4. You're welcome!
5. I'd love to.

2

Invitation

Dear **Lora**

You are invited to my **birthday** party!

Date: **Saturday 14th April / April 14**

Time: **3 p.m.**

Place: 5, Mill street,
in the **garden**

Dress code: dress up as **pirates**

From: **Sebby**

3
1. **Hi,** Sebby. **This is** Lora. **Thank** you very much for your invitation. I'd be very happy to come to your party. **See you** on Saturday!
2. It's me Alex. I'm very **sorry** I can't come to your **party.** I'm **busy** on Saturday: I'm babysitting my little brother. But I wish you a very happy **birthday.**

9 L'expression de l'avenir (p. 22)

1
1. My little brother **will be** eight years old next month.
2. I**'ll see** you tomorrow, Luke!
3. It's cold and grey. It**'s going to snow.**
4. The train leaves in five minutes, so we**'ll arrive** in London in two hours.
5. Harrison **won't come** with us if he's still sick.
6. My mum is fed up with her old car. She **is going to get** a new car soon.

On emploie **be going to** en **3.** car on prédit qu'il va neiger à partir de ce qu'on voit et en **6.** pour parler de l'intention de la maman.

2
1. I'm not going to lie to you…
2. We're going to take the first train…
3. … it isn't going to rain ou it's not going to rain.
4. You aren't going to pass ou you're not going to pass…
5. She's going to have an accident…
6. You're going to regret it…

3
1. Will Kelly be with her parents?
2. Is it going to take a long time?
3. Are we going to listen to Mike's presentation?
4. Are they going to play basketball?
5. Am I going to be late?
6. Will it be dark when we get there?

4
1. I'm going to redecorate my room.
2. I'll be a vet one day.
3. I won't play rugby next year.
4. It's going to rain. Don't forget your umbrella!
5. I'll arrive at noon if it doesn't snow.

10 À la maison (p. 24)

1
1. the chimney
2. the roof
3. the (sash) window
4. the bay window
5. the porch
6. the door
7. the step(s)
8. the lawn ou the garden

2
1. a wardrobe → the bedroom
2. a bath → the bathroom
3. a desk → the study
4. a settee, a sofa → the living room
5. a chest of drawers → the bedroom
6. a basin → the bathroom

3
a bulb – a remote control –
a piece of furniture – a desk – a fireplace –
a shower

4
1. CARPET
2. MIRROR
3. WARDROBE
4. BRUSH
5. ATTIC
6. BEDSIDE TABLE
7. BOOKCASE
8. CELLAR
Il relie les pièces : **CORRIDOR** (le couloir).

11 Les pronoms personnels (p. 26)

1
1. **It** is red.
2. **He** is red.
3. **She** is in red.

2
1. I love him.
2. Can I say hello to them?
3. I think we can now get on it.
4. "Who is she?"
5. I can't shut it!
6. Can you hear it?

3
1. My granddad is coming tonight. **He** is coming with my uncle.
2. My aunt is sick. **She** can't come tonight.
3. This computer is new. I bought **it** last month.
4. My neighbours' cars are old. **They** want to sell **them.**
5. Elizabeth is my cousin. Do you want to meet **her**? **She** is very nice.
6. Oh, **it** is late. Wake up, Mike! **It** is 7 o'clock.

Nice to meet you, Robin Hood

EN ANGLETERRE AU TEMPS DE RICHARD CŒUR DE LION

Laurent DEDRYVER

Jean-Marc PAU

Nice to meet you, Robin Hood

EN ANGLETERRE AU TEMPS DE RICHARD CŒUR DE LION

SCÉNARIO
Laurent DEDRYVER

ILLUSTRATION
Jean-Marc PAU

Hatier

Nice to meet you, Robin Hood

Dreamland, a beautiful village in England.

Two Boys aged 13 live there. They are close friends. Danny is rather adventurous...

... whereas Peter is quiet and shy

Danny's father is a scientist. One day he builds a machine that he keeps in a workshop in his garage. Danny knows his father has a secret.

One night while everybody is sleeping Danny steals the keys from his father...

... and discovers a stange machine.

He decides to share his secret with his best friend.

He doesn't know yet that the machine is going to take him and his friend into a great adventure where they will meet a famous hero...

1 Danny's Secret

Danny a un secret. À qui le dire sinon à son meilleur ami, Peter?

@))) www.bescherelle.com

Hi, Peter! How are you?

Fine, thanks, and you?

Not too bad.

Listen, I've got a secret to tell you.

A secret? What is it?

Well, there's a workshop in my garage and... inside there's a strange machine.

What kind of machine is it?

I don't know, Peter. It's my father's, probably

Please, come with me and see it, Pete.

OK, Dan, but just see it, right?

Quiz

1. Danny and Peter are at school. ☐ True. ☐ False.
2. They are friends. ☐ True. ☐ False.
3. Peter is reading when Danny arrives. ☐ True. ☐ False.
4. Danny is pleased to meet Peter. ☐ True. ☐ False.
5. Danny wants Peter to follow him. ☐ True. ☐ False.

2 A Strange Machine

Danny a convaincu Peter de venir voir la machine de son père. Juste la voir...

@)) www.bescherelle.com

It's locked, but I've got the key.

Look! It has got a steering-wheel, a door and windows.

Has it got an engine, too?

I don't know but it hasn't got any wheels.

It's very strange.

Your father's a scientist, isn't he? So ask him what it is.

No! It's a secret. He doesn't know that I've got his key, and I've got a better idea.

A better idea?

Look! If we press one of the buttons on each side of the steering-wheel, perhaps...

No, it's too dangerous, Dan, and I haven't got much time.

Oh, come on, Pete!

All right, but be careful.

Quiz

1. The workshop door is open. ☐ True. ☐ False.

2. Everybody has this kind of machine at home. ☐ True. ☐ False.

3. This machine is a modern car. ☐ True. ☐ False.

4. Danny is a very inquisitive boy. ☐ True. ☐ False.

5. Peter is not in a hurry. ☐ True. ☐ False.

3 Testing the Machine

Une fois devant la machine, il est tentant de monter dedans ! C'est fait !

@))) www.bescherelle.com

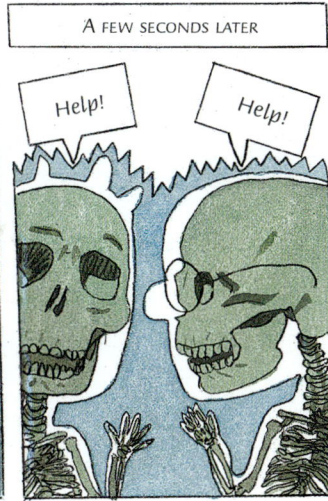

Look! There are some letters and figures. What are they for?

I haven't a clue.

AD and BC... Press one of them, Pete.

Are..., are you sure?

Don't worry and listen to me, it's not dangerous.

OK! but I'm a bit frightened.

Now, the figures. 1, 1, 9, 2... What does it mean?

Don't press the button, Dan.

Why not?

Wait for your dad and ask him what this machine is. He can help us.

STEERING WHEEL AND FASTEN THE SEAT BELTS

Too late! What? Fasten your seat belts!

A FEW SECONDS LATER

Help!

Help!

Quiz

1. Peter and Danny know what the machine is. ☐ True. ☐ False.
2. Danny only wants to have a look at it. ☐ True. ☐ False.
3. Peter is afraid of it. ☐ True. ☐ False.
4. Danny tries to reassure him. ☐ True. ☐ False.
5. The machine asks them to do something. ☐ True. ☐ False.

4 An Unknown Place

La machine s'est mise en route ! Mais pour où ?

(@)) www.bescherelle.com

Where are we?

Ouch! My head.

We're in a forest. A beautiful forest.

There's no forest next to our village, is there?

No, there isn't... Hem, phone your parents, Pete. Mine aren't at home this afternoon.

OK!

My phone is not working, Danny. Give me yours, please.

Oh, my God! It's not working either. I don't like that at all!

Look over there, Dan. Can you see that man on his horse? His clothes are weird.

You're right, Pete. He's probably a bit crazy.

Hey you! Look, Pete! He's got a bow in his hand. He's got a sword and some arrows, too.

You're right. He's totally mad.

Quiz

1. Danny and Peter wake up in Dreamland. ☐ True. ☐ False.
2. Danny can't join his parents. ☐ True. ☐ False.
3. Peter's phone doesn't work. ☐ True. ☐ False.
4. The man is a neighbour of theirs. ☐ True. ☐ False.
5. He does not look normal. ☐ True. ☐ False.

5 The Rider

Voilà Danny et Peter dans une forêt inconnue face à un type bizarre.

@)) www.bescherelle.com

Er, excuse me, sir. We're lost and...

Who are you, kids? Are you spying on me?

Spying on you? We're looking for our village.

Here in Sherwood!? What are you doing here, boys?

Either he is laughing at us or he's completely nuts.

Our names are Peter and Danny and we're lost. Can you please tell us where we are?

Robin Hood!?

Oh, I understand, you're an actor and...

I'm not an ... actor! I'm Robin Hood.

... you're acting in a film, aren't you?

Of course I can! You are in Sherwood forest and my name's Robin Hood.

Look, Peter! Here come the other actors. It's funny, isn't it?

Quiz

1. Danny and Peter are talking to a friend. ☐ True. ☐ False.
2. They are asking him for information. ☐ True. ☐ False.
3. The man says he is a famous outlaw. ☐ True. ☐ False.
4. Danny and Peter think he is joking. ☐ True. ☐ False.
5. The man is a real actor. ☐ True. ☐ False.

6 More Riders

Peter et Danny sont perplexes. Sont-ils tombés sur le tournage d'un film ?

www.bescherelle.com

Who are these kids, Robin?

I don't know, Tuck.

Robin, Tuck... I think I'm dreaming.

I don't understand what's happening, Dan.

Look at their clothes!

But we always dress like this! How do you usually dress, I mean when you don't act?

What do they mean, Robin?

I don't know but it isn't safe to stay here.

Don't worry, Robin! The sheriff and his men never leave Nottingham for Sherwood.

Yes, Pete! My father's machine is actually a time machine!! We are in 1192! This man's the real Robin Hood!

Oh no!

Robin ..., Tuck..., Sherwood..., Nottingham... the sheriff..., our phones that don't work... I think I understand, Pete.

?!

How exciting! Hooray!!

Quiz

1. The newcomers are the rider's friends.   ☐ True. ☐ False.

2. They look surprised by Danny and Peter's clothes. ☐ True. ☐ False.

3. Peter understands what is happening.   ☐ True. ☐ False.

4. The scene takes place in the 21st century.   ☐ True. ☐ False.

5. Danny is pleased with what is happening.   ☐ True. ☐ False.

7 The Proof

Robin des Bois a conduit Peter et Danny dans son camp pour les interroger.

www.bescherelle.com

Well, kids! Who are you and where are you from?

We are Peter and Danny. We live in Dreamland.

And where are your horses?

We haven't got any horses.

So, how do you travel?

Well, we actually live in the 21st century and thanks to a time machine that my father ...

The 21st century? A time machine? Stop it! What do you mean?

Yes, look, Sir Robin! Here is some proof: a mobile phone and a watch.

And ... and this is a ... a pair of glasses.

OH!

All this is very puzzling, Robin. What do you think of that?

Well, we'll talk about that tomorrow after the attack on the convoy.

Great! An attack!!

Oops!!

Quiz

1. Robin wants to know a lot of things about the two boys. ☐ True. ☐ False.

2. Robin and his companions are not surprised to see a mobile phone. ☐ True. ☐ False.

3. Robin is not sure that the boys tell the truth. ☐ True. ☐ False.

4. Danny and Peter can prove that they are not lying. ☐ True. ☐ False.

5. Peter does not want to take part in the attack. ☐ True. ☐ False.

8 Attack in the Forest

Robin n'est pas tout à fait convaincu. Mais pour l'instant place à l'action !

 @))) www.bescherelle.com

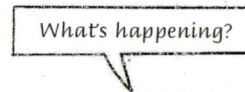

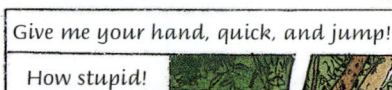

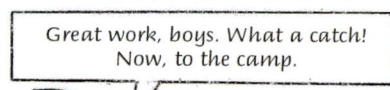

It's frightening, isn't it, Dan?

No, it's quite exciting. Look! There's the convoy!

Oh no!

Boys, stay here for the moment and watch!

Stop!

What's happening?

You must pay a tax to go through this forest, or we're going to take your gold.

Give me your hand, quick, and jump!

How stupid!

Great work, boys. What a catch! Now, to the camp.

Look, Pete! Two of them are trying to escape.

Quiz

1. When the convoy arrives, the two boys are pleased. ☐ True. ☐ False.

2. Robin asks Danny and Peter to intercept the convoy. ☐ True. ☐ False.

3. Danny notices that two of their enemies are trying to run away. ☐ True. ☐ False.

4. Robin congratulates the two boys on their bravery. ☐ True. ☐ False.

5. After the attack they all go to Nottingham. ☐ True. ☐ False.

9 The New Heroes

Pete et Dan ont fait prisonniers deux hommes du convoi. C'est la gloire !

@)) www.bescherelle.com

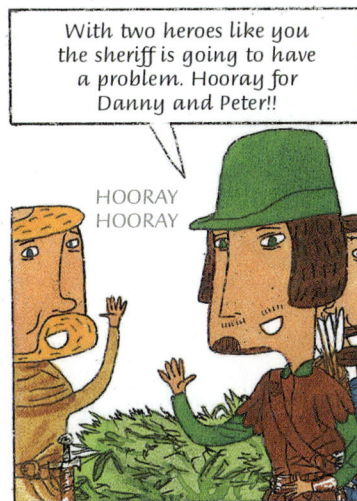

Hooray for Danny and Peter! You were so brave.

HOORAY HOORAY

Thank you! We're pleased to help you. It was nothing at all.

Whoever you are, boys, we're glad to count you as our friends.

What do you think of that, Pete?

Er..., er...., I'm delighted to hear that. Really.

Well, as far as you're concerned, we advise you to leave for Nottingham and tell the sheriff that this forest is forbidden to all those who share his views.

Danny, Peter, here are some clothes you must wear here. They were mine when I was young.

Thank you very much, Sir Robin.

With two heroes like you the sheriff is going to have a problem. Hooray for Danny and Peter!!

HOORAY HOORAY

Quiz

1. Robin and his companions are pleased with the two boys. ☐ True. ☐ False.

2. They decide to keep their victims prisoners. ☐ True. ☐ False.

3. Robin thinks the boys must wear green clothes. ☐ True. ☐ False.

4. Danny and Peter agree with Robin's decision. ☐ True. ☐ False.

5. They are not a threat to the sheriff. ☐ True. ☐ False.

Sword Handling and Archery

Pete et Dan font maintenant partie de la bande. Mais ils ont encore à apprendre...   @)) www.bescherelle.com

Danny, Peter, now that you're outlaws you must learn how to use a bow and a sword.

Oh yes! Good idea, Sir Robin.

Yes, good idea!

How did you defend yourselves at home? Did you have any weapons?

Of course not! In the 21st century weapons are forbidden.

Forbidden? So before coming here you lived in a place where cruel sheriffs and thieves could rob you of everything you had and...

No, Sir Robin. Things are different now. There are no more cruel sheriffs because... they are elected by the people and thieves go to jail. We don't need to use weapons at all.

What a wonderful place! But here we need our weapons. Tuck! Much!

Here we are, Robin.

These two kids are eager to be part of our group. Can you teach them how to aim at a target and fight with a sword?

Of course we can. Two more skillful outlaws is what we need in this forest.

Quiz

1. Now Peter seems to enjoy life in the woods.   ☐ True.   ☐ False.

2. There are no differences between the 12th and the 21st centuries.   ☐ True.   ☐ False.

3. Robin and his men can't live without swords or bows.   ☐ True.   ☐ False.

4. Robin doesn't like the place where Danny and Peter live.   ☐ True.   ☐ False.

5. Tuck and Much are chosen to be Danny and Peter's teachers.   ☐ True.   ☐ False.

11 Cards and Chess Games at Sherwood

Pete et Dan ont appris à tirer à l'arc et à manier l'épée. Place aux jeux !

@))) www.bescherelle.com

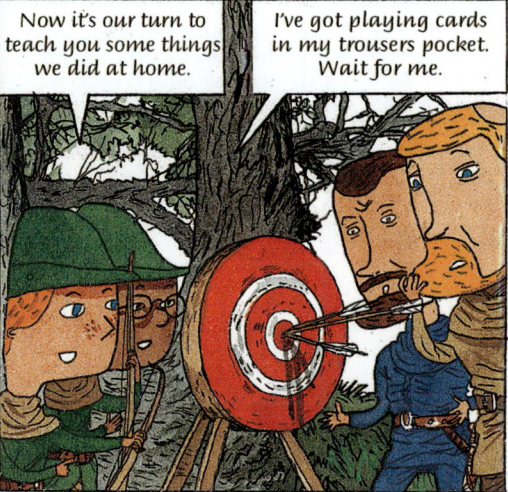

Now it's our turn to teach you some things we did at home.

I've got playing cards in my trousers pocket. Wait for me.

While I was looking for the cards I found this, too. It's my electronic chess game.

The aim of this game is to capture the king.

Ours is to set him free. Ha! Ha!

HA! HA! HA!

HOURS LATER…

How interesting!

That was great!

Can we play again?

No, while you were playing someone arrived and I want to introduce our friends to this person. Danny, Peter, can you follow me, please?

Sure, Sir Robin.

And stop calling me "Sir". Robin is enough.

Quiz

1. Danny and Peter want their new friends to play with them. ☐ True. ☐ False.

2. Peter only found playing cards in his trousers. ☐ True. ☐ False.

3. The outlaws enjoyed the games. ☐ True. ☐ False.

4. Danny and Peter know who the newcomer is. ☐ True. ☐ False.

5. Robin is pleased when the boys call him "sir". ☐ True. ☐ False.

The Arrival of Maid Marian

Quelqu'un vient d'arriver au camp : c'est l'heure des présentations.

@))) www.bescherelle.com

Hem, Danny, Peter... Here's the person I want to introduce you to. This is Marian.

Pleased to meet you.

We're pleased to meet you, too. This is Peter and I'm Danny.

Marian lives in Nottingham and she sometimes comes to Sherwood to give us some precious information about what's happening there.

Yes, and I must tell you that the sheriff is angry, angrier than ever before, because of the latest attack.

He intends to capture you, Robin, to prove that you aren't as dangerous as some pretend.

I'm more dangerous than he says.

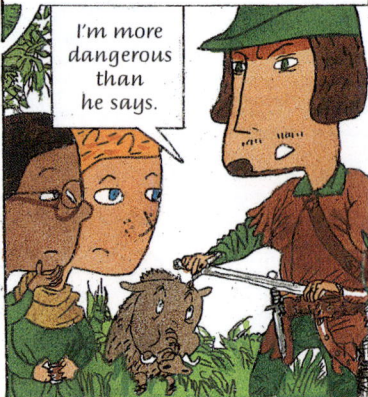

I know, Robin, but be careful, darling. He's so cruel.

Don't worry, sweetheart. He is arrogant but he isn't as clever as he thinks. Now return to Nottingham and take care.

Good luck, and see you soon.

As soon as I hear about anything important.

Quiz

1. Marian is Robin's sister. ☐ True. ☐ False.
2. She lives in another forest close to Nottingham. ☐ True. ☐ False.
3. She has a message for Robin. ☐ True. ☐ False.
4. She doesn't think the sheriff is dangerous. ☐ True. ☐ False.
5. She intends to come back to Sherwood. ☐ True. ☐ False.

13 The Most Beautiful Lady on Earth

Marian, l'amie de Robin, a fait grande impression sur Danny. Amoureux ?

@)) www.bescherelle.com

Quiz

1. Danny thinks Marian is lovely. ☐ True. ☐ False.

2. She has got other qualities. ☐ True. ☐ False.

3. Marian plays a part in the conflict between Robin and the sheriff. ☐ True. ☐ False.

4. Danny and Peter know how to return to 21st century England. ☐ True. ☐ False.

5. They are worried about their parents. ☐ True. ☐ False.

14 The Silver Arrow

Il y a du neuf à Nottingham. Le shérif prépare sa revanche !

@)) www.bescherelle.com

Robin! Where's Robin?

Hello, Marian! What's wrong with you? You look upset.

I have some important information for Robin!

Here I am, my love.

Robin! The sheriff is going to organise an archery tournament just because he hopes to capture you!

He hasn't got any brains. I'm not going to get caught that easily...

Well, don't go, Robin. Nor any of your men.

What's the reward for the winner?

Please don't go, Robin! It's a trap. There are soldiers everywhere in Nottingham.

I must go to prove to him that I'm not a coward and that I'm more clever than he is.

But first I need some new clothes, especially a hood to cover my face.

Oh, Robin, I think that you have no brains either!

A silver arrow.

Quiz

1. Marian looks relaxed when she gets to Sherwood. ☐ True. ☐ False.
2. There is going to be a tournament in Nottingham. ☐ True. ☐ False.
3. Robin thinks the sheriff is a fool. ☐ True. ☐ False.
4. He does not want to take part in the tournament. ☐ True. ☐ False.
5. He needs a hood because it is raining. ☐ True. ☐ False.

15 The Archery Tournament

Robin n'a pas suivi les conseils de Marian : il participe au concours de tir à l'arc.

www.bescherelle.com

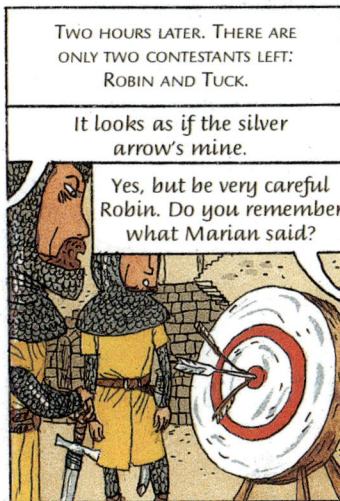

TWO DAYS LATER IN NOTTINGHAM.

We must be very careful, Tuck. If someone recognizes us we are done for.

Yes, look at all those soldiers on alert. Come on, the tournament is going to start.

Where's the sheriff? I can't see him anywhere.

He must be somewhere in the crowd. Look, there he is!

THE TOURNAMENT STARTS.

He looks worried. Something is bothering him.

Nobody can aim better than you, Robin.

Maybe you can, Tuck.

TWO HOURS LATER. THERE ARE ONLY TWO CONTESTANTS LEFT: ROBIN AND TUCK.

It looks as if the silver arrow's mine.

Yes, but be very careful Robin. Do you remember what Marian said?

Congratulations, sir. CATCH HIM!! It's probably Robin Hood!!

Quiz

1. Robin wants to pass unnoticed. ☐ True. ☐ False.

2. There are not many soldiers. ☐ True. ☐ False.

3. The sheriff is not present at the tournament. ☐ True. ☐ False.

4. Tuck does not think Robin can win. ☐ True. ☐ False.

5. In the end, Robin is the best bowman in the kingdom. ☐ True. ☐ False.

16 Two Courageous Kids

Robin a gagné le concours mais le piège du shérif se referme.

Run, Robin!

I'm not your prisoner yet!

Catch them, quick! They can't escape!

Follow me to the ramparts.

Here come the soldiers. It's over, Robin.

No, we still have our weapons, so we can fight.

Robin! Tuck! Can you hear us?

Look down there, Tuck! I can't believe it! Are you ready to jump?

That's our only chance, isn't it?

What are you doing here, boys? You're supposed to be at Sherwood, aren't you?

We didn't want to leave you alone in Nottingham. So we decided to follow you while nobody was paying attention to us and... here we are! Now hurry!

Quiz

1. The sheriff asks the soldiers to arrest Robin and Tuck. ☐ True. ☐ False.

2. Tuck thinks they can't escape. ☐ True. ☐ False.

3. The two outlaws are pleased to see Danny and Peter. ☐ True. ☐ False.

4. Someone asked Danny and Peter to go and help Robin and Tuck. ☐ True. ☐ False.

5. They all hurry up because of the soldiers. ☐ True. ☐ False.

Richard Must Be Set Free

Peter et Danny ont sauvé Robin des griffes du shérif. Mais il reste à faire...

www.bescherelle.com

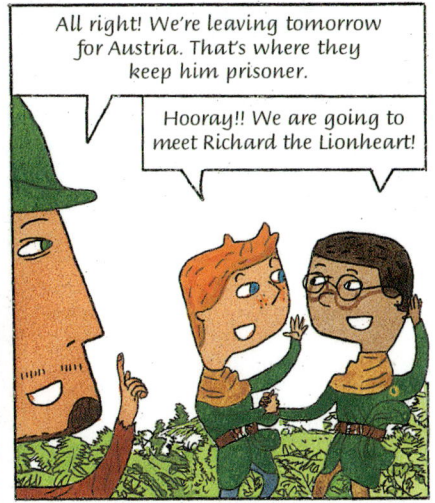

Once again your help was vital, boys. Thank you very much for what you did. Without you ...

Don't mention it, Robin. It was a real pleasure.

But now we must think about a way of freeing Richard.

You're right. We have enough money to pay the ransom that his kidnappers demand.

Richard must be set free and the sheriff has to pay for all his crimes!

The people of England must be ruled by a good king. Long live King Richard!

LONG LIVE KING RICHARD!!

Well, when are we leaving?

We? You don't have to come if ...

Yes, we're coming. We could help.

All right! We're leaving tomorrow for Austria. That's where they keep him prisoner.

Hooray!! We are going to meet Richard the Lionheart!

Quiz

1. Robin is cross with Danny and Peter. ☐ True. ☐ False.

2. The sheriff is a criminal. ☐ True. ☐ False.

3. The two boys think England does not deserve a bad king. ☐ True. ☐ False.

4. They want to stay in the forest while Robin is away. ☐ True. ☐ False.

5. Richard is in jail in England. ☐ True. ☐ False.

18 The Ransom

Robin a décidé de verser la rançon et de délivrer Richard Cœur de Lion.

@))) www.bescherelle.com

I know that King Richard is prisoner in a castle that is at the top of a hill.

Oh! Poor Richard! I'll be so happy to see him again. I hope he is well.

Hey! Look over there in the distance! It's the castle.

Here we are at last!

Who are you and what do you want?

We are here to pay the ransom for our king. Open your doors!

First, let me see what you call a ransom. I can't see anything and don't tell me it's all in your pockets. Ha! Ha! Ha!

How clever! Bring the prisoner!

I wonder what he looks like.

I can't imagine either.

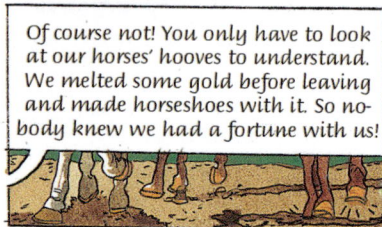

You're free at last, your Highness.

I owe you so much. But how about leaving this place once and for all? I'm looking forward to seeing England again.

Of course not! You only have to look at our horses' hooves to understand. We melted some gold before leaving and made horseshoes with it. So nobody knew we had a fortune with us!

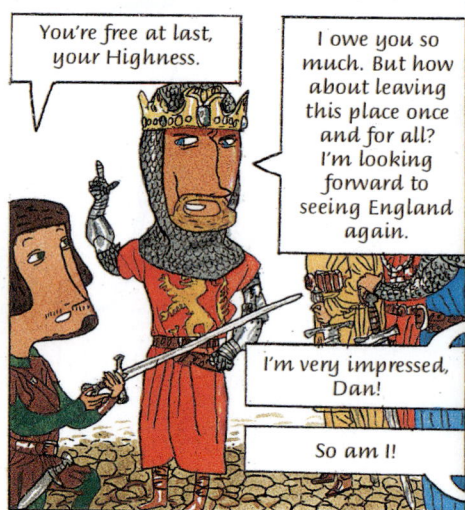

I'm very impressed, Dan!

So am I!

Quiz

1. Friar Tuck hopes Richard is in good shape. ☐ True. ☐ False.
2. The kidnappers want to see the ransom before releasing their prisoner. ☐ True. ☐ False.
3. The ransom was hidden in bags. ☐ True. ☐ False.
4. During the journey the outlaws had problems with some thieves. ☐ True. ☐ False.
5. Richard doesn't want to linger near the castle. ☐ True. ☐ False.

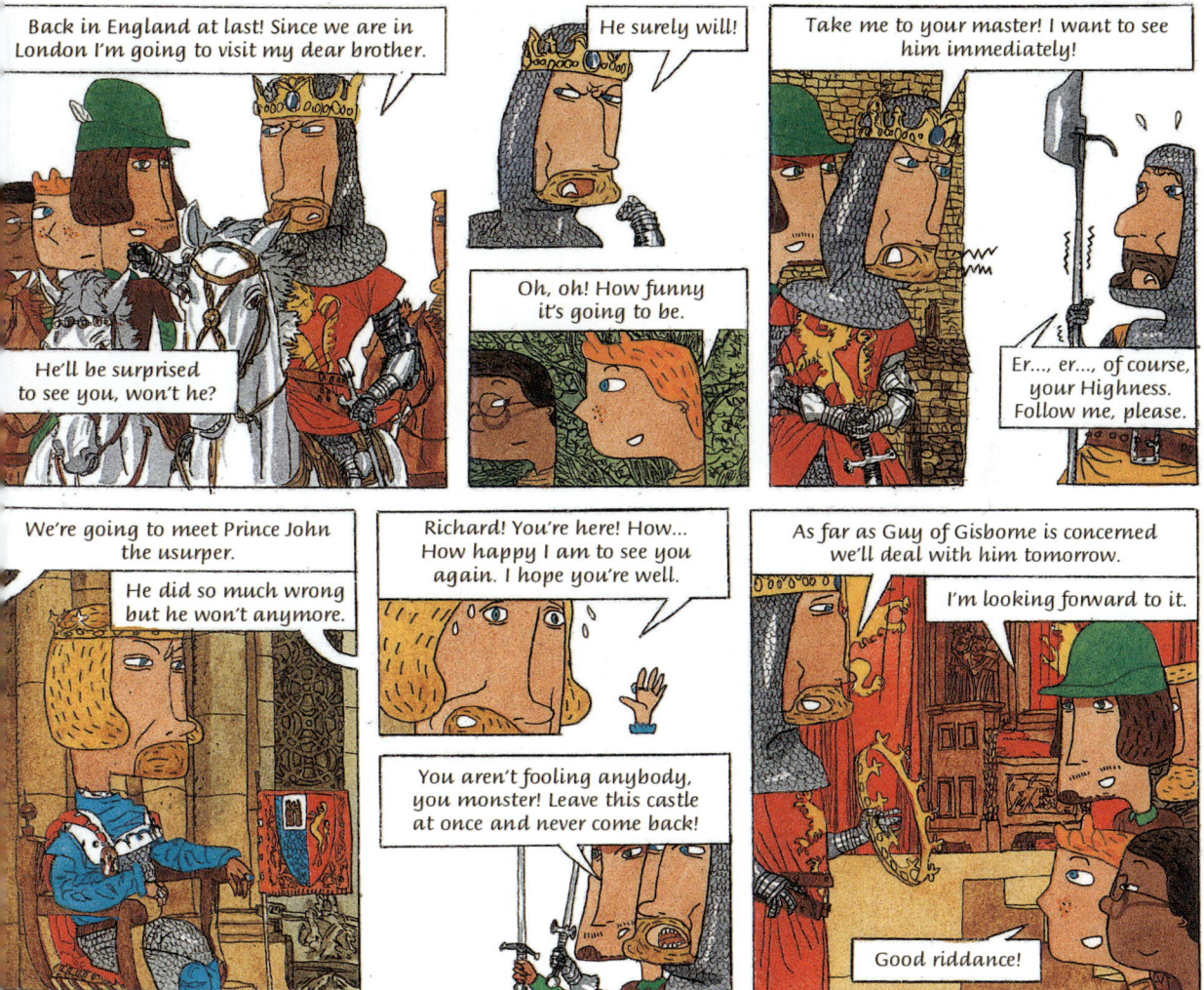

19 An Unexpected Visit

Richard Cœur de Lion est libre et revient en Angleterre.

Back in England at last! Since we are in London I'm going to visit my dear brother.

He'll be surprised to see you, won't he?

He surely will!

Oh, oh! How funny it's going to be.

Take me to your master! I want to see him immediately!

Er..., er..., of course, your Highness. Follow me, please.

We're going to meet Prince John the usurper.

He did so much wrong but he won't anymore.

Richard! You're here! How... How happy I am to see you again. I hope you're well.

You aren't fooling anybody, you monster! Leave this castle at once and never come back!

As far as Guy of Gisborne is concerned we'll deal with him tomorrow.

I'm looking forward to it.

Good riddance!

Quiz

1. Prince John is a relative of Richard's. ☐ True. ☐ False.
2. He is pleased to see his brother again. ☐ True. ☐ False.
3. He was not a bad king. ☐ True. ☐ False.
4. He can visit Richard whenever he likes. ☐ True. ☐ False.
5. Richard wants Prince John to deliver a message to Guy of Gisborne. ☐ True. ☐ False.

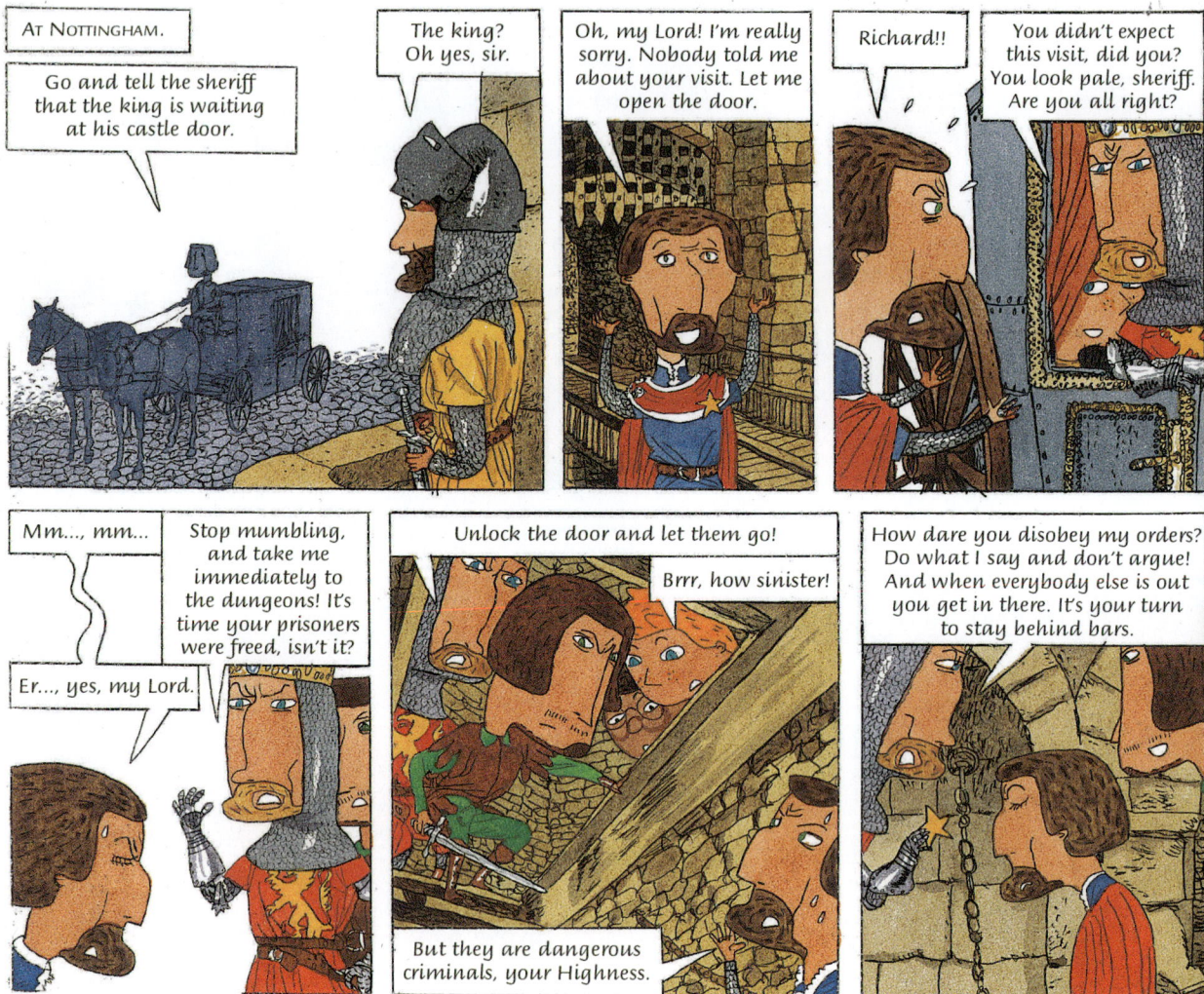

20 The Sheriff in Jail

Richard est de nouveau roi d'Angleterre. Au tour du shérif de payer !

AT NOTTINGHAM.

Go and tell the sheriff that the king is waiting at his castle door.

The king? Oh yes, sir.

Oh, my Lord! I'm really sorry. Nobody told me about your visit. Let me open the door.

Richard!!

You didn't expect this visit, did you? You look pale, sheriff. Are you all right?

Mm..., mm...

Stop mumbling, and take me immediately to the dungeons! It's time your prisoners were freed, isn't it?

Er..., yes, my Lord.

Unlock the door and let them go!

Brrr, how sinister!

But they are dangerous criminals, your Highness.

How dare you disobey my orders? Do what I say and don't argue! And when everybody else is out you get in there. It's your turn to stay behind bars.

Quiz

1. The sheriff thinks Prince John, not Richard, is in the stagecoach. ☐ True. ☐ False.
2. He is not very surprised to see his brother. ☐ True. ☐ False.
3. Richard wants the prisoners to be released. ☐ True. ☐ False.
4. The sheriff is pleased to unlock the prisoners. ☐ True. ☐ False.
5. To punish Prince John, Richard intends to banish him from Nottingham. ☐ True. ☐ False.

I Knight You

Voilà le shérif en prison. Pour les fidèles du roi Richard, que d'honneurs...

www.bescherelle.com

Robin, Danny, Peter and you, the merry men, I asked you here today because I want to congratulate you on all that you did while I was a prisoner.

We only did what we thought was good for England.

And you did it well. Thanks to you England is free again and its people can hope for a better future..., and so can I!

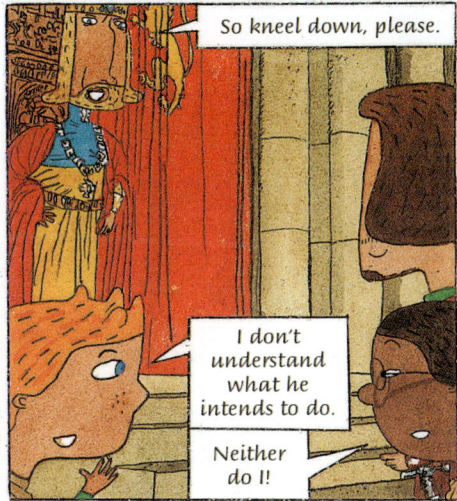

So kneel down, please.

I don't understand what he intends to do.

Neither do I!

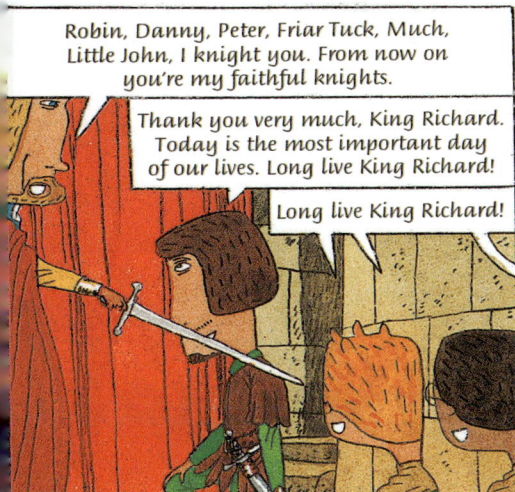

Robin, Danny, Peter, Friar Tuck, Much, Little John, I knight you. From now on you're my faithful knights.

Thank you very much, King Richard. Today is the most important day of our lives. Long live King Richard!

Long live King Richard!

I'm not looking forward to going back home after such a wonderful day.

I am! Just to tell our friends everything about our adventures.

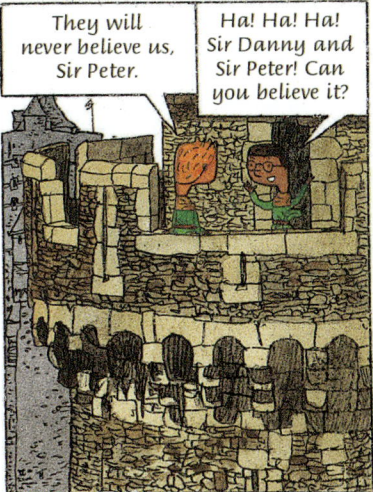

They will never believe us, Sir Peter.

Ha! Ha! Ha! Sir Danny and Sir Peter! Can you believe it?

Quiz

1. Richard is grateful to Robin and his men. ☐ True. ☐ False.
2. Danny and Peter know what is going on. ☐ True. ☐ False.
3. The outlaws are rewarded by their king. ☐ True. ☐ False.
4. Robin considers this day as very important. ☐ True. ☐ False.
5. The boys will not have difficulty explaining their adventures. ☐ True. ☐ False.

22 Robin and Marian Get Married

Danny et Peter ont été faits chevaliers. Et la fête continue !

@)) www.bescherelle.com

Tuck! Are you ready? Everybody's waiting for you.

I'm coming, don't worry. Wow! The castle is packed.

Forget the audience and do your job as well as you can.

Hm..., we are assembled here, in this chapel to celebrate the wedding of Marian and Robin...

How lucky he is!

Ha! Ha! Still in love with the most beautiful lady on earth?

Marian, do you take Robin as your husband?

I do.

Robin, do you take Marian as your wife?

I do.

I now pronounce you man and wife. Let the party begin!

Stop laughing at me! I'm not in love at all.

Ha! Ha! Ha! I'm not sure. Look at yourself, you look so sad.

HOORAY! HOORAY! HOORAY!

Forget Marian, Dan. She's Robin's forever now. Ha! Ha! They're looking at each other like two lovebirds.

How funny!

Quiz

1. Friar Tuck is late.   ☐ True. ☐ False.

2. There are not many people in the castle.   ☐ True. ☐ False.

3. Maid Marian is going to marry Robin.   ☐ True. ☐ False.

4. Peter looks very serious during the ceremony.   ☐ True. ☐ False.

5. The wedding is a success.   ☐ True. ☐ False.

23 A Newcomer

Voilà Marian et Robin mariés. Mais qui arrive ?

www.bescherelle.com

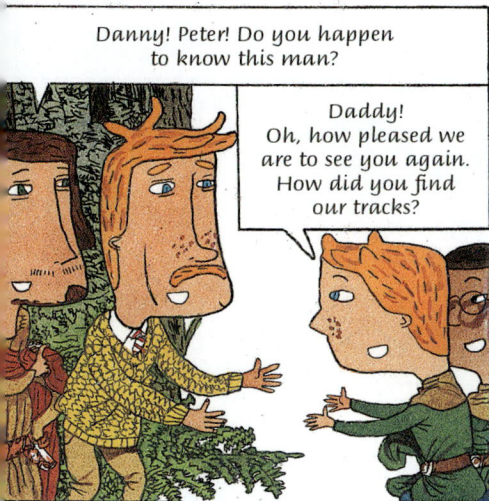

Danny! Peter! Do you happen to know this man?

Daddy! Oh, how pleased we are to see you again. How did you find our tracks?

Well, that wasn't easy at all. When you used the time machine it wasn't ready yet, that's why you ended up in Nottingham instead of staying in Dreamland.

Moreover the machine was supposed to travel with you but fortunately it didn't! In fact it needed some adjustments. So I set to work. Everybody was putting pressure on me to finish it.

It took me several days to fix it. When it was over I tried a few destinations because I didn't know where you were, and eventually I landed here last night. But, how are you?

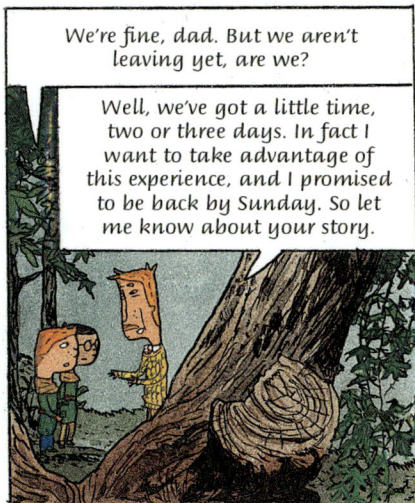

We're fine, dad. But we aren't leaving yet, are we?

Well, we've got a little time, two or three days. In fact I want to take advantage of this experience, and I promised to be back by Sunday. So let me know about your story.

OK, but first let us introduce you to our friends, Robin Hood, Friar Tuck, Much, Lady Marian...

That's unbelievable!

Quiz

1. Dan's father is angry with the boys. ☐ True. ☐ False.
2. It was difficult for him to find them. ☐ True. ☐ False.
3. The time machine is out of order now. ☐ True. ☐ False.
4. They must leave immediately. ☐ True. ☐ False.
5. Danny is looking forward to returning home. ☐ True. ☐ False.

24 Last Day at Sherwood

Mr Trainor, le père de Danny, a retrouvé les deux garçons.
Il faut songer au retour...

@)) www.bescherelle.con

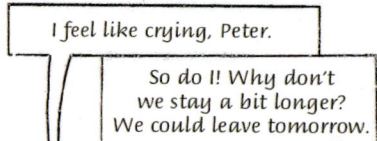

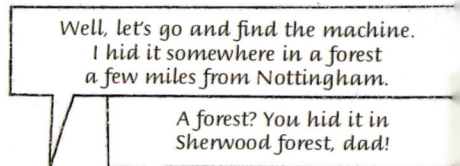

Robin, Tuck, Much, Little John..., we must leave. Unfortunately our stay with you is over.

We know and we'll remember you. You proved to be great heroes. How about taking a souvenir with you?

Oh yes! And we'll leave you er..., my watch!

And my chess game!

In exchange for my bow and my silver arrow.

And my knife. And my club.

That's wonderful! But won't you need them?

We hope not! Now that peace is back weapons are useless.

I feel like crying, Peter.

So do I! Why don't we stay a bit longer? We could leave tomorrow.

No, it will be the same tomorrow.

Danny! Peter! Are you ready?

Well, let's go and find the machine. I hid it somewhere in a forest a few miles from Nottingham.

A forest? You hid it in Sherwood forest, dad!

Where you had your wonderful adventures. We'll go with you!

Quiz

1. Robin, his companions and the boys exchange gifts as proof of their friendship. ☐ True. ☐ False.

2. Robin intends to make another bow. ☐ True. ☐ False.

3. Danny and Peter are pleased to leave the 12th century. ☐ True. ☐ False.

4. They both think they can wait until the following day. ☐ True. ☐ False.

5. Mr Trainor does not know exactly where the time machine is. ☐ True. ☐ False.

25 Back Home

'est l'heure du départ... Mais où est la machine ?

www.bescherelle.com

IN THE FOREST.

Well, there must be somewhere an enormous oak, taller than all the others. The machine is hidden behind it.

An enormous oak? I see what you mean. Look over there, is that the tree you were talking about?

I suppose so. It was so dark when I arrived.

Where did you sleep by the way?

I slept under the stars. That's why I've got a ... a... ATISHOO... a cold.

Bless you! Ha! Ha! Ha!

This is the place where I landed last night. Look at the broken branches which are strewn all over the ground. Oh! Here it is!

What a strange thing! How curious!

Dear companions, we must split up. It's time we returned home but we'll never forget you.

We won't forget you either but you have to go back to your family and friends. Our regards to the future generations.

Ready? Ready, dad.

So, we're off!

Ready, Mr Trainor.

BYE BYE BYE

Quiz

1. Mr Trainor did not hide the machine.   ☐ True.   ☐ False.
2. Mr Trainor spent the previous night in a barn.   ☐ True.   ☐ False.
3. Robin and his companions are amazed by the machine.   ☐ True.   ☐ False.
4. The two boys feel very sad.   ☐ True.   ☐ False.
5. Robin has a message for his descendants.   ☐ True.   ☐ False.

26 The Destruction of the Machine

La machine a reconduit les voyageurs au XXIᵉ siècle. Servira-t-elle encore ?

@)) www.bescherelle.co

Hey, daddy! What are you doing?

Well, I'd like to keep the machine but I don't think it's a good idea.

Why not? We could use it again.

That's the problem, boys. I don't want you or anybody else to use it again.

I don't understand, dad. Everybody would like to have such a machine at home, wouldn't they?

I know, but I don't want to be responsible for losing someone.

I mean, what if the machine breaks down after someone uses it? Who knows what can happen with such experiments?

I suppose you're right. Do you want us to help you?

Yes, sure! It's pretty simple. You just have to press the black button.

I'll do it. I feel like I'm doing something wrong but I must do it.

I think so too, Dan. Go ahead!

Don't have any regrets, boys. And always remember your experience as one of the most wonderful in your life!

Quiz

1. Mr Trainor intends to build another machine. ☐ True. ☐ False.

2. He thinks his machine could have problems. ☐ True. ☐ False.

3. The machine cannot be destroyed. ☐ True. ☐ False.

4. Mr Trainor thinks Danny and Peter's experience was unique. ☐ True. ☐ False.

5. Danny refuses to destroy the machine himself. ☐ True. ☐ False.

Corrigés des quiz

1 Danny's Secret
1. False. 2. True. 3. True. 4. True. 5. True.

2 A Strange Machine
1. False. 2. False. 3. False. 4. True. 5. False.

3 Testing the Machine
1. False. 2. False. 3. True. 4. True. 5. True.

4 An Unknown Place
1. False. 2. True. 3. True. 4. False. 5. True.

5 The Rider
1. False. 2. True. 3. True. 4. True. 5. False.

6 More Riders
1. True. 2. True. 3. False. 4. False. 5. True.

7 The Proof
1. True. 2. False. 3. True. 4. True. 5. True.

8 Attack in the Forest
1. False. 2. False. 3. True. 4. True. 5. False.

9 The New Heroes
1. True. 2. False. 3. True. 4. True. 5. False.

10 Sword Handling...
1. True. 2. False. 3. True. 4. False. 5. True.

11 Cards and Chess Games...
1. True. 2. False. 3. True. 4. False. 5. False.

12 The Arrival of Maid Marian
1. False. 2. False. 3. True. 4. False. 5. True.

13 The Most Beautiful Lady...
1. True. 2. True. 3. True. 4. False. 5. True.

14 The Silver Arrow
1. False. 2. True. 3. True. 4. False. 5. False.

15 The Archery Tournament
1. True. 2. False. 3. False. 4. False. 5. True.

16 Two Courageous Kids
1. True. 2. True. 3. True. 4. False. 5. True.

17 Richard Must Be Set Free
1. False. 2. True. 3. True. 4. False. 5. False.

18 The Ransom
1. True. 2. True. 3. False. 4. False. 5. True.

19 An Unexpected Visit
1. True. 2. False. 3. False. 4. False. 5. False.

20 The Sheriff in Jail
1. True. 2. False. 3. True. 4. False. 5. False.

21 I Knight You
1. True. 2. False. 3. True. 4. True. 5. False.

22 Robin and Marian Get Married
1. True. 2. False. 3. True. 4. False. 5. True.

23 A Newcomer
1. False. 2. True. 3. False. 4. False. 5. False.

24 Last Day at Sherwood
1. True. 2. False. 3. False. 4. False. 5. True.

25 Back Home
1. False. 2. False. 3. True. 4. True. 5. True.

26 The Destruction of the Machine
1. False. 2. True. 3. False. 4. True. 5. False.

Nice to meet you, Robin Hood

LAURENT DEDRYVER

JEAN-MARC PAU

**EN ANGLETERRE
AU TEMPS
DE RICHARD
CŒUR DE LION**

Danny est bien curieux... et bien imprudent !
Il embarque son copain Peter dans une machine
étrange fabriquée par son père. Mais la machine
n'est pas terminée et c'est le début d'incroyables
aventures... qui nous mènent dans la forêt
de Sherwood, avec Robin des Bois.

4166731

7. <u>Jack and I</u> are cousins, so **we** have the same grandparents. They give **us** a lot of presents.
8. Don't use this <u>towel</u>. I want to wash **it**.
9. I can't find <u>my bag</u>. Do you know where **it** is?

12 Sounds, sounds, sounds... @)) (p. 28)

1 "You're listening to radio 841. Our guest today is Richard Parkinson. Richard is a photographer for a famous magazine. Richard, thanks so much for joining us."
"Thank <u>you</u>."
"Richard, you will be following the Queen in Australia next month. Your job will be to take pictures of the people she will meet – presidents, ministers, celebrities… Is that right?"
"Yes. My job is to take photos and I think it is a great opportunity for me, and then in September I will go to Africa, I will see the people there. I am very lucky."
"Send us your comments on the Queen's tour to Australia – and Richard Parkinson going with her – on our website: www.radio841.org.co.uk!"

1. Name of the radio station: **radio 841.**
2. Name of the guest: **Richard Parkinson.**
3. His job: **photographer.**

The guest is going to accompany the **Queen** to **Australia** and will go to **Africa** in **September.**

☑ It's an opportunity. ☑ It's great.

2 Hi! I'm Tom! I live in Fleet Street. My house is a Victorian house, it has a red roof and a green door. There are three windows, my bedroom is upstairs. We have a small garden.

Maison c.

3 inhabited • comfortable • tidy • attractive • patient • formal • friendly • polite

4 uninhabited • uncomfortable • untidy • unattractive • impatient • informal • unfriendly • impolite

On remarque que l'ajout d'un préfixe (**un-**, **in-**, **im-**) ne déplace pas l'accent de mot.

5
☑ seek	☐ sick	☐ chick	☑ cheek
☐ ship	☑ sheep	☑ team	☐ Tim
☐ pick	☑ peak	☐ fill	☑ feel
☑ theme	☐ thin	☑ seen	☐ sin

Le son /ɪ/ est produit par la lettre **i** suivie d'une **consonne.**
Les voyelles **-ee** (et parfois **-ea**) se prononcent toujours /iː/.

6
1. parking
2. ☑ camping
3. ☑ thing
4. jumping
5. casting
6. ☑ dancing
7. footing

8. ☑ meeting
9. ☑ pudding
10. jogging
11. ☑ smoking
12. ☑ building

7
1. could – ~~shout~~ – should
2. ridiculous – generous – ~~about~~
3. ~~enough~~ – bought – fought
4. ~~although~~ – drought – cloud
5. ~~enormous~~ – proud – scout
6. found – ~~tough~~ – out

13 Comparatifs et superlatifs (p. 30)

1
1. She's **happier** than her cousins.
2. Pat was **more interested** in the story than Craig.
3. This dress is **nicer** than yours.
4. Your results are **better** this year.
5. Which is **bigger**: Big Ben or the Eiffel Tower?
6. My dog is a Chihuahua. He is **smaller** than your cat.
7. Are cats **more clever** than dogs?
8. Your cat is **fatter** than mine.
9. This film is **worse** than the one we saw last week.

2
1. the fastest
2. the best
3. the tallest
4. the most intelligent
5. the most interesting
6. the worst
7. the happiest

3 **Comparatifs :** better, nicer, larger, faster, taller, slimmer, funnier

Superlatifs : (the) worst, (the) nicest, (the) fattest, (the) longest, (the) prettiest, (the) quickest

Comparatif mystère : **MORE AMUSING**

14 Dans la vie de tous les jours (p. 32)

1 On Saturday, I usually <u>got</u> [**get**] up at 9.
I have <u>lunch</u> [**breakfast**] and then, I <u>clear</u> [**brush**] my teeth.
After that, I <u>wash</u> [**have**] a shower and <u>get dress</u> [**get dressed**].
Then, I <u>make</u> [**do**] my homework and learn my lessons.
At noon, I have <u>dinner</u> [**lunch**]. In the afternoon, I <u>listen</u> **to** music or watch television.

2
1. Mum
2. Alice
3. Jack
4. Dad

3 I often do the housework. (Je fais souvent le ménage.)

15 Les articles et les démonstratifs (p. 34)

1
1. They are building **a** new school here.
2. "What's **an** enemy?" "It's the opposite of **a** friend."
3. I can give you **an** answer in **an** hour.
4. Do they have **a** house in Scotland?
5. I have **an** uncle who lives in San Francisco.
6. It's **a** book about **an** honest person persecuted by **a** horrible colleague.

Phrase 6 : dans **honest**, on ne prononce pas le **h** et donc on dit : **an honest person** mais dans **horrible**, on prononce le **h** et donc on dit : **a horrible colleague.**

2
1. **The** maths teacher has a cold.
2. **The** computer is broken.
3. Which do you prefer: Ø tea or Ø coffee?
4. Where's **the** teapot?
5. I like Ø tea but I prefer Ø chocolate!
6. Could you please shut **the** door?
7. Ø money doesn't grow on trees!

3 I have **a** new friend. He's **a** hamster. He is **the** best companion I could dream of. He lives in **an** elegant little house. I built **the** house myself. It's made of Ø wood. Ø life is so beautiful when I'm with him.

4
1. **This** chair is very comfortable.
2. **That** mountain is so high! [montagne vue de loin]
3. **These** letters are for me, not for you.
4. I don't like **those** trousers.

16 Les sports (p. 36)

1
1. football (GB) / soccer (US)
2. American football (GB) / football (US)
3. horse riding
4. hiking
5. swimming
6. skating

Sois cohérent! Si tu choisis l'anglais américain, choisis systématiquement le deuxième mot proposé pour le football ! Il ne faut pas mélanger anglais britannique et anglais américain !

2

athletics	running, a team, a coach
hiking	a footpath, walking, the forest
tennis	a net, running, a team, a ball, hitting the ball, a racket, a coach

3
1. When you win, you can win a trophy.
2. If an athlete breaks a record, he or she can become a world champion.
3. You need very good equipment when you do competitive sports.
4. At the Olympic Games, athletes can win a gold medal.

4 gagner : **win** – médaille : **medal** – long : **long** – jouer : **play** – entraîneur : **coach** – concourir : **compete** – court : **court** – sauter : **jump**

C	O	M	P	E	T	E
O	O	J	E	H	P	G
A	W	U	I	D	L	N
C	I	M	R	G	A	O
H	N	P	H	T	Y	L

Mot mystère : **HIGH**

17 Les possessifs et le génitif (p. 38)

1
1. Sally's hair
2. the Prince's house
3. my parents' bosses
4. our friends' video games
5. this girl's schoolbag
6. these girls' schoolbags

2
1. Do you like her mother?
2. Her sisters are going to the ball.
3. Where are his keys?
4. She was their friend.
5. Her grandparents were ill.
6. Can you imagine their house?

3
1. These kids have a lot of toys. I like **their** toys.
2. He has a new computer. I like **his** computer.
3. Camilla has an old bike. I like **her** bike.
4. This flower has a strange colour. I like **its** colour.

4
1. Malika has a new house. I visited **Malika's house**.
2. John and Sandra have five cousins. I know **John and Sandra's cousins**.
3. My parents have a new car. I like **my parents' car**.
4. My friend collects stamps. I love looking at **my friend's stamps**.

18 Sounds, sounds, sounds... @)) (p. 40)

1 lion /ˈlaɪən/ • unicorn /ˈjuːnikɔːn/ • crown /kraʊn/ • bread /bred/.
L'intrus est : plum

2 Le **h** ne se prononce pas dans **hour** et **honour**, qui sont précédés du déterminant **an** (et non **a**).

3

	/əʊ/ comme dans n**o**te	/uː/ comme dans m**oo**n
old	☒	
shoe		☒
know	☒	
do		☒
go	☒	
school		☒

4 1. I don't like **this**. ☑ this /ðɪs/
2. **These** things belong to me! ☑ **these** /ðiːz/
3. **This** man is a genius! ☑ **this** /ðɪs/
4. **These** flowers are beautiful. ☑ **these** /ðiːz/
5. Do you prefer **these**? ☑ **these** /ðiːz/

5 Phrase **3**. He isn't just a singer, he is the best singer of the 21st century!

6

/ð/	/θ/
them, there, clothes, then, theirs	tooth, think, thing, thin, theatre, thirsty, three, Thursday, through

7

/æ/ comme c**a**t	/eɪ/ comme m**a**ke	/ɪ/ comme s**i**x	/aɪ/ comme f**i**ve
bad, rat, mad	late, place, made, break, game	fish, bit, sit, thin, win	nine, site, bite, white, try, night

19 **Les mots interrogatifs (p. 42)**

1 1. "**Who** is in the hall?"
2. "**What**'s that?"
3. "**Where** are you going, Sue?"
4. "**What** time is it?"
5. "**When** are you leaving, Sue?"
6. "**Why** are you smiling?"
7. "**Whose** mobile phone is this?"

2 1. Where are you going tomorrow?
2. Why aren't you with your brother?
3. Who is going with you?
4. What did you do yesterday?
5. When did you go to Scotland?
6. Why do you go to school by bus?

3 1. **Why** is Jim going to Japan next week?
2. **What** does Leslie love?
3. **When** does his cat wake him up?
4. **Where** do the Walkers live?
5. **Who** are the Walkers?
6. **Whose** bike is this?
7. **Who** has got ou **Who**'s got problems?

20 **Trouver son chemin (p. 44)**

1 1. cinema 2. car park 3. chemist's 4. sports store
5. shoe shop 6. clothes shop
7. restaurant 8. bookshop

2 1. on ≠ **under**
2. in front of ≠ **behind**
3. inside ≠ **outside**
4. to the north ≠ **to the south**
5. to the left ≠ **to the right**
6. out of ≠ **into**
7. close (to) ≠ **far (from)**
8. to go up ≠ **to go down**

3 1. Can you tell me the way to the museum?
Yes, of course, it's easy.
2. How far is it from here? About 2 miles.
3. Where is it? In High Street, next to the town hall.
4. How can I get there? You can walk up the street or take the number 9 bus.

21 *A lot of, much, many, some, any* et *no* (p. 46)

1 1. Are there **many** stars on the American flag?
2. Kelly is sorry but she doesn't have **much** time.
3. I didn't buy **many** postcards.
4. Have you got **much** money with you?

Dans toutes les phrases ! **A lot of** (beaucoup de) est suivi d'un nom singulier ou pluriel et s'emploie dans tous les types de phrases.

2 1. We don't have **any** money.
Nous n'avons pas d'argent.
2. I need **some** money to buy **some** pens.
J'ai besoin d'argent pour acheter des stylos.
3. Did you get **any** mail today?
As-tu reçu du courrier aujourd'hui?
4. Mike hasn't got **any** friends.
Mike n'a pas d'amis.
5. Did you make **any** friends during your holiday?
Tu t'es fait des amis pendant tes vacances ?

Some est utilisé dans la phrase 2 car elle est à la forme affirmative.

3 1. My cat ate no vegetables.
2. We took no pictures.
3. I have no friends.
4. She has no respect for my work.

22 **La nature (p. 48)**

1 This picture represents a village at the foot of a **cliff**, on top of which there is a yellow **lighthouse**. It is on a small **island**. There is a **sand beach** where people can bathe in summer.

2 1. heather : **a moor**
2. a hill : **the countryside**
3. water : **a lake**
4. sand : **a beach**
5. a fir : **the mountain**

3 phare : **lighthouse** – buisson : **bush** – eau : **water**
– blé : **wheat** – plage : **beach** – bois : **wood** –
haie : **hedge** – chêne : **oak** – mer : **sea** –
herbe : **grass** – feuille : **leaf**

L	I	G	H	T	H	O	U	S	E
O	A	K	C	L	E	A	F	S	W
W	H	E	A	T	D	S	O	A	O
W	A	T	E	R	G	E	R	R	O
H	S	U	B	C	E	A	K	G	D

Mot mystère : **ROCK**

4 1. branches
2. leaves
3. a lake (ou a loch)
4. a river
5. the tide
6. a chestnut tree

23 Les prépositions et les particules (p. 50)

1 1. I love looking **at** the moon.
2. I'm looking **for** my keys.
3. Does this house belong **to** your parents?
4. I'm not talking **to** you.
5. I'm talking **about** Rhoda.
6. They are looking **for** a new apartment.
7. How much did you pay **for** this software?

2 1. I'm waiting **for** the train to Glasgow.
2. What are you thinking **about** ou **of**?
3. Rex always obeys Ø my sister, not me.
4. We're writing a letter **to** Grandma.
5. I don't remember Ø your cousin.
6. We entered Ø the house in silence.
7. I trust Ø every person I meet.

3 1. Who are you waiting for?
2. What is Luke thinking about?
3. Who is Martha talking to?
4. What are the pupils writing on?

4 1. Don't give up the fight!
Particule. Le verbe **give** signifie « donner » ; le
verbe **give up** signifie « abandonner ».
2. Give this letter to her.
Préposition. Il s'agit du verbe **give**. La préposition
to introduit le complément du verbe.
3. The cat is sleeping on my bed.
Préposition. Il s'agit du verbe **sleep**. La préposition **on** introduit le lieu sur lequel dort le chat.
4. You should go on.
Particule. Le verbe **go** signifie « aller » ; le verbe
go on signifie « continuer ».

24 Sounds, sounds, sounds... @)) (p. 52)

1 "Excuse me, can you tell me the way to the
Museum please?"
"Of course! You turn left and then right at
the traffic lights. You go straight on past the
supermarket and take the second street on your
left. At the next crossroads, you still go straight
on and there you are! The museum is on your
left."
Le musée correspond à la lettre B.

2 phon<u>e</u>tic • scien<u>ti</u>fic • ex<u>o</u>tic • acad<u>e</u>mic •
opti<u>mi</u>stic • sar<u>ca</u>stic • organic • synthetic •
historical • practical • illogical • identical

La syllabe accentuée se situe juste avant
le suffixe **-ic.**

3 1. How many biscuits do you want? ↘
2. Where does your sister live? ↘
3. Are you busy right now? ↗
4. Can anybody help me? ↗
5. Who is your favourite singer? ↘
6. Is he going to move to Australia? ↗
7. Who is your source of inspiration? ↘

Quand la question commence par un pronom
interrogatif (**how, where**...), l'intonation est
descendante. Quand elle commence par un
auxiliaire, elle est **montante**.

4 1. Why can't you forget him? ☑ irritation
2. Why can't you forget him? ☑ curiosité
3. You'd better not use a dictionary for this
translation. ☑ bienveillance
4. You'd better not use a dictionary for this
translation. ☑ ton autoritaire
5. My brother is supposed to stay at home during
the holidays. ☑ tristesse
6. My brother is supposed to stay at home during
the holidays. ☑ joie

5 sit – <u>seat</u> • <u>bird</u> – bed • <u>bean</u> – bin • bun – <u>burn</u>
• <u>read</u> – rid • <u>far</u> – fat • still – <u>steal</u> • black – <u>blue</u>
• pot – <u>port</u> • gin – <u>jeans</u>

6 1-c aubergine
2-b pollution
3-g lasso
4-d periscope
5-a Bible
6-f littoral
7-h eglantine
8-e article

4 Écoute maintenant ces mêmes mots précédés d'un préfixe (**un-**, **in-**, ...) et souligne la syllabe accentuée.

uninhabited	uncomfortable	untidy	unattractive
impatient	informal	unfriendly	impolite

Compare avec tes réponses à l'exercice 3. Que remarques-tu ? ....
....

5 Dans les paires suivantes, coche le mot dont le son **i** est long : /iː/.

☐ seek   ☐ sick   ☐ chick   ☐ cheek

☐ ship   ☐ sheep   ☐ team   ☐ Tim

☐ pick   ☐ peak   ☐ fill   ☐ feel

☐ theme   ☐ thin   ☐ seen   ☐ sin

Que remarques-tu ici?

Le son /ɪ/ est produit par la lettre **i** suivie d'une ....

Les voyelles **-ee** (et parfois **-ea**) se prononcent toujours ....

6 Écoute et compare : le premier mot de chaque paire est anglais, le deuxième est français.

ring / dingue   song / tong   sang / exsangue

> **Rappel**
> En anglais, la terminaison en **-ng** /ŋ/ se prononce de telle sorte que le **-g** final s'entend à peine.

Écoute ensuite les mots suivants et coche ceux qui sont prononcés en anglais.

1. ☐   3. ☐   5. ☐   7. ☐   9. ☐   11. ☐

2. ☐   4. ☐   6. ☐   8. ☐   10. ☐   12. ☐

Les mots cochés sont maintenant prononcés à la suite. Répète-les.

7 Écoute ces groupes de trois mots qui comportent tous les lettres **ou** et raye dans chaque groupe l'intrus qui se prononce différemment.

1. could – shout – should

2. ridiculous – generous – about

3. enough – bought – fought

4. although – drought – cloud

5. enormous – proud – scout

6. found – tough – out

13 Comparatifs et superlatifs

Il y a deux façons de comparer : avec les <u>comparatifs</u>, pour comparer deux éléments (plus que) ou avec les <u>superlatifs</u>, pour comparer plus de deux éléments (le plus).

✳ Les comparatifs de supériorité (plus... que...)

● On utilise les comparatifs de supériorité pour comparer deux éléments.
Lucy is **more** competent **than** you.
Lucy est plus compétente que toi.

👁 L'équivalent de « que » après les comparatifs est **than**. Il ne faut surtout pas utiliser **that** dans ce cas !

● Les comparatifs de supériorité se forment de deux façons.

adjectif <u>court</u> (une seule syllabe)	adjectif +-**er**	tall → tall**er** (plus grand)
adjectif <u>long</u> (plus d'une syllabe)	**more** + adjectif	intelligent → **more** intelligent (plus intelligent)

Oranges are sweet**er than** lemons.
Les oranges sont plus sucrées que les citrons.

New York is **more expensive than** Chicago.
New York est plus cher que Chicago.

● Les adjectifs de deux syllabes qui se terminent par **-y** font leur comparatif en **-ier** :
happy (heureux) → **happier** (plus heureux).

👁 Certains comparatifs sont irréguliers : **good** (bon) → **better** (meilleur), **bad** (mauvais) → **worse** (pire).

✳ Les superlatifs (le plus ...)

● On utilise les superlatifs pour comparer un élément à un ensemble.
Rex is **the most intelligent** dog in the neighbourhood.
Rex est le chien le plus intelligent du quartier.

● Les superlatifs se forment de deux façons.

adjectif <u>court</u> (une seule syllabe)	**the** + adjectif + -**est**	tall → the tall**est** (le plus grand)
adjectif <u>long</u> (plus d'une syllabe)	**the most** + adjectif	intelligent → the **most** intelligent (le plus intelligent)

👁 Certains superlatifs sont irréguliers : **good** (bon) → **the best** (le meilleur), **bad** (mauvais) → **the worst** (le pire).

Exercices

1 **Complète ces phrases avec un comparatif de supériorité.**

I'm .... (tall) than you. → I'm taller than you.

1. She's .... (happy) than her cousins.

2. Pat was .... (interested) in the story than Craig.

3. This dress is .... (nice) than yours.

4. Your results are .... (good) this year.

5. Which is .... (big): Big Ben or the Eiffel Tower?

6. My dog is a Chihuahua. He is .... (small) than your cat.

7. Are cats .... (clever) than dogs?

8. Your cat is .... (fat) than mine.

9. This film is .... (bad) than the one we saw last week.

> **Coup de pouce** Quand un adjectif se termine par **1** voyelle + **1** consonne, on double la consonne !

2 **Ton copain Jack n'est pas dans la même classe que toi. Complète ses questions avec un superlatif.**

In your class :

1. Who is the .... (fast) runner?

2. Who is the .... (good) pupil?

3. Who is the .... (tall) boy?

4. Who is the .... (intelligent) girl?

5. Who is the .... (interesting) pupil?

6. Who is the .... (bad) pupil?

7. And finally who is the .... (happy) of them all?

3 **Trouve dans la grille, écrits dans tous les sens, les comparatifs et superlatifs suivants.**

Au comparatif : good – nice – large – fast – tall – slim – funny
Au superlatif : bad – nice – fat – long – pretty – quick

M	R	E	T	T	E	B	T	O
Q	U	I	C	K	E	S	T	T
F	R	R	E	A	E	S	S	A
U	E	M	U	C	E	E	S	L
N	T	S	I	T	I	L	R	L
N	S	N	T	T	I	E	I	E
I	A	A	T	M	G	N	G	R
E	F	E	M	R	E	C	I	N
R	R	E	A	W	O	R	S	T
P	R	L	O	N	G	E	S	T

> **Coup de pouce**
> Attention, certaines lettres sont utilisées deux fois.

Avec les lettres restantes, remises dans l'ordre, tu écriras un autre comparatif, synonyme de funnier :

__ __ __ __

__ __ __ __ __ __ __

14 Dans la vie de tous les jours

@))) On schooldays, I **get up** at 6:30 a.m. First, I **have a shower** and **get dressed.**
After **breakfast, I brush my teeth, comb my hair** and I **leave home** at 7:35 because
I **take the bus** at 7:40.

Les jours d'école, je me lève à 6 h 30. D'abord, je prends une douche et je m'habille. Après le petit déjeuner,
je me brosse les dents, je me coiffe et je quitte la maison à 7 h 35 car je prends le bus à 7 h 40.

✹ In the morning (le matin)

- to wake* /eɪ/ up : se réveiller
- to get* up : se lever
- to have* breakfast : prendre le petit déjeuner
- to have* a shower /ʃaʊə/ : prendre une douche
- to brush /brʌʃ/ one's teeth /iː/ : se brosser les dents

- to get* dressed : s'habiller
- to comb /kəʊm/ one's hair : se coiffer
- to leave* /iː/ home : quitter la maison
- to go* to school : aller à l'école
- to take* the bus/the underground : prendre le bus/le métro

✹ At school (à l'école)

- to get* to school : arriver à l'école
- to be* late : être en retard
- to be* on time : être à l'heure
- to be* early : être en avance

- to have* a lesson/a class : avoir un cours
- to listen (to) : écouter
- to have* lunch : déjeuner
- to get* (back) home : rentrer à la maison

✹ After school (après l'école)

- to have* tea : prendre le thé, goûter
- to do* one's 'homework : faire ses devoirs
- to learn* /ɜː/ : apprendre
- to watch 'television : regarder la télévision
- to play : jouer
- to phone : téléphoner
- to text : envoyer des SMS
- to go* out : sortir

- to have* dinner : dîner
- to undress : se déshabiller
- pyjamas (pl.) : un pyjama
- to have* a wash : faire sa toilette
- to go* to bed : aller au lit
- to read* a story : lire une histoire
- to fall* asleep : s'endormir
- to sleep* : dormir

✹ Doing the housework (faire le ménage)

- to tidy (up) : ranger, faire du rangement
- tidy /taɪdi/ : rangé, soigné
- 'messy : en désordre
- to make* one's bed : faire son lit
- to hoover (GB), to vacuum /vækjuːm/ : passer l'aspirateur
- to clean /iː/ : nettoyer

- to set* the table : mettre la table
- to clear the table : débarrasser la table
- to do* the washing-up : faire la vaisselle
- to do* the cooking : faire la cuisine
- to do* the shopping : faire les courses
- to take* the bin out : sortir la poubelle

1 Il y a huit erreurs dans ce paragraphe. Souligne-les puis écris la correction.

On Saturday, I usually got up at 9. I have lunch and then, I clear my teeth.

....

After that, I wash a shower and get dress.

....

Then, I make my homework and learn my lessons. At noon, I have dinner.

....

In the afternoon, I listen music or watch television.

....

- usually /juːʒʊəli/ : habituellement

2 Dans notre famille, nous nous répartissons les tâches ménagères et, chaque semaine, chacun a une série de corvées à faire. Trouve de qui il s'agit dans chacune des phrases ci-dessous.

Dad			✓		✓
Mum		✓		✓	
Alice		✓			
Jack	✓				

This week, Dad or Mum or Alice or Jack:

1. has to do the shopping and wash the clothes. ....
2. has to help this person with the shopping. ....
3. has to vacuum all the rooms in the house. ....
4. has to cook and take the bin out. ....

3 Peux-tu déchiffrer ce message codé ? Il parle de corvée !

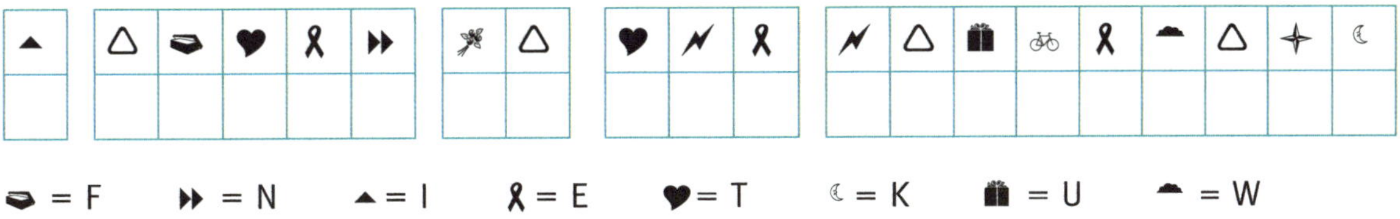

Coup de pouce Tu dois trouver sans avoir tous les codes !

15 Les articles et les démonstratifs

L'article **a** est proche des articles « un, une ». L'article **the** se traduit par
« le, la, les » mais « le, la, les » ne se traduit pas toujours par **the** ! Parfois on
n'utilise pas d'article en anglais là où on en utilise un en français.
Il existe deux démonstratifs : **this** (pluriel : **these**) et **that** (pluriel : **those**).

✳ L'article a

On emploie **a** /ə/ devant un son de consonne et **an** /ən/ devant un son de voyelle.

a /ə/ + son de consonne	**an** /ən/ + son de voyelle
a boy (un garçon)	**an** animal (un animal)
a girl (une fille)	**an** idea (une idée)
a small dog (un petit chien)	**an** intelligent person (une personne intelligente)

> ◉ La lettre **h** se prononce en anglais. C'est une consonne. On dit donc **a house**
> (une maison), **a habit** (une habitude).
> Mais **h** ne se prononce pas dans **hour**. On dit donc **an hour**.

✳ L'article the

● On emploie **the**, comme « le, la, les », pour parler d'une personne ou d'un objet identifié.
The teacher is already in **the** classroom.
La prof est déjà dans la salle de classe. [Il s'agit de la prof que nous connaissons, toi et moi.]
Hurry up! **The** bus is coming.
Dépêche-toi ! Le bus arrive. [Il s'agit du bus que nous allons prendre, toi et moi.]

● Quand « le, la, les » désigne une **généralité**, on n'emploie pas **the**. On dit parfois qu'on
utilise « l'article zéro » dans ce cas.

I like _tea.   _Bread is made with _flour.
J'aime **le** thé.   **Le** pain est fait avec de **la** farine.

✳ Les démonstratifs

Les démonstratifs servent principalement à montrer quelque chose.

	singulier	pluriel
proche	this /ðɪs/	these /ðiːz/
non proche	that /ðæt/	those /ðəʊz/

This letter is for you. But **these** letters are for me.
Cette lettre est pour toi. Mais ces lettres sont pour moi. [les lettres que j'ai dans les mains]
Look at **that** motorbike! And look at **those** cars!
Regarde cette moto ! Et regarde ces voitures ! [les véhicules que je montre du doigt]

Exercices

1 Remplis les blancs avec **a** ou **an**. Justifie ta réponse pour la phrase 6.

1. They are building .... new school here.

2. "What's .... enemy?" "It's the opposite of .... friend."

3. I can give you .... answer in .... hour.

4. Do they have .... house in Scotland?

5. I have .... uncle who lives in San Francisco.

6. It's .... book about .... honest person persecuted by .... horrible colleague.

Dans la phrase 6, ...

2 Article **the** ou pas d'article ? Emploie le symbole Ø pour l'absence d'article.

1. .... maths teacher has a cold. I hope I won't catch it!

2. .... computer is broken. We should buy a new one.

3. Which do you prefer: .... tea or .... coffee?

4. Where's .... teapot? I can't find it anywhere.

5. I like .... tea but I prefer .... chocolate!

6. Could you please shut .... door?

7. .... money doesn't grow on trees!

3 Dans le SMS de Lucy tous les articles ont sauté. Rétablis-les.

I have .... new friend. He's .... hamster. He is .... best companion I could dream of. He lives in .... elegant little house. I built .... house myself. It's made of .... wood. .... life is so beautiful when I'm with him.

> ■ wood : du bois

4 Complète les légendes à l'aide d'un démonstratif en t'aidant des dessins.

1. .... chair is very comfortable.

2. .... mountain is so high!

3. .... letters are for me, not for you.

4. I don't like .... trousers.

16 | Les sports

@)) "Do you want to go **hiking** tomorrow, John?" "No, Dad, thanks. My friends and I are **going for a bike ride.** We have discovered a new **footpath.**"

« Tu veux venir marcher demain, John ? – Non, papa, merci. Avec mes copains, on va faire une randonnée à vélo. On a trouvé un nouveau chemin. »

✸ Team sports (les sports d'équipe)

- a team /tiːm/ : une équipe
- practice /ɪ/, training : l'entraînement
- a coach : un entraîneur
- a ball /bɔːl/ : un ballon, une balle
- football (GB), soccer (US) : le football
- American football (GB), football (US) : le football américain
- 'rugby : le rugby

- cricket : le cricket
- a match : un match
- to play : jouer
- a goal : un but
- a 'goalkeeper : un gardien de but
- a referee /refəˈriː/ : un arbitre
- to score a goal /gəʊl/ : marquer un but

✸ Competition (la compétition)

- to do* sport : faire du sport
- to practice /ɪ/ : s'entraîner
- a sportsman, a sportswoman (pl. : -men/ -women) : un sportif, une sportive
- an athlete /ˈæθliːt/ : un athlète
- a champion : un champion
- a compe'tition : un concours
- to compete : concourir
- an event /ɪˈvent/ : une épreuve
- a contest /ˈkɒntest/ : une rencontre sportive
- to win* : gagner

- to beat*, to defeat : battre
- 'victory : la victoire
- a cup : une coupe
- to lose* /luːz/ : perdre
- the Olympic Games, the O'lympics : les Jeux olympiques
- gold : l'or
- silver : l'argent
- bronze : le bronze
- a 'medal : une médaille
- to break* a 'record : battre un record

✸ Activities (les activités sportives)

- swimming : la natation
- a swimming pool : une piscine
- a swimsuit : un maillot de bain
- table tennis, ping-pong : le ping-pong, le tennis de table
- squash /skwɒʃ/ : le squash
- a court : un court
- a 'racket : une raquette
- to hit* the ball : frapper la balle
- a net : un filet

- hiking /aɪ/ : la randonnée
- a (public) footpath : un sentier (public)
- to ride* /raɪd/ : monter (à cheval, à vélo)
- horse riding : l'équitation
- to jump : sauter
- a bike /aɪ/ : un vélo
- to run* : courir
- the ice rink : la patinoire
- skating : le patinage

1 Nomme en anglais les sports représentés par ces dessins.

1. ....   4. ....

2. ....   5. ....

3. ....   6. ....

2 Complète le tableau en faisant correspondre chaque sport aux mots qui peuvent lui être associés. Certains mots peuvent être utilisés deux fois.

a net – a footpath – running – a team – a ball – walking – hitting the ball – the forest – a racket – a coach

athletics	....
hiking	....
tennis	....

■ athletics : l'athlétisme

3 Fais correspondre le début de la phrase avec la fin qui convient.

1. When you win, ...

2. If an athlete breaks a record, ...

3. You need very good equipment ...

4. At the Olympic Games, ...

● ... athletes can win a gold medal.

● ... when you do competitive sports.

● ... he or she can become a world champion.

● ... you can win a trophy.

4 Retrouve dans la grille la traduction des mots suivants.

gagner – médaille – long – jouer – entraîneur – concourir – court (de tennis) – sauter

C	O	M	P	E	T	E
O	O	J	E	H	P	G
A	W	U	I	D	L	N
C	I	M	R	G	A	O
H	N	P	H	T	Y	L

Avec les lettres restantes, tu pourras former le mot dont voici l'indice :

If you can jump __ __ __ __ , you are an athlete.

17 Les possessifs et le génitif

Voici les déterminants possessifs, avec les pronoms personnels correspondants. Les déterminants possessifs désignent généralement qui possède quoi.

pronoms personnels sujets	I	you	he/she/it	we	they
déterminants possessifs	**my**	**your**	**his/her/its**	**our**	**their**

✸ Les déterminants possessifs

● Il n'y a qu'un seul déterminant possessif par personne. Compare avec le français.

my bag　　　　　　　　　**my** car　　　　　　　　　**my** emails
mon sac　　　　　　　　　**ma** voiture　　　　　　　　**mes** e-mails

your bag　　　　　　　　　**your** car　　　　　　　　　**your** emails
ton sac ou **votre** sac　　　**ta** voiture ou **votre** voiture　　**tes** e-mails ou **vos** e-mails

● En anglais, on accorde le déterminant possessif avec le **possesseur**. Quand on veut traduire « son, sa, ses », il faut donc savoir si on parle d'une femme **(her)**, d'un homme **(his)** ou d'un objet **(its)**.

Look at Jane. I love **her** shirt.　　　　　Look at Richard. I love **his** shirt.
Regarde Jane. J'adore **sa** chemise.　　　　Regarde Richard. J'adore **sa** chemise.

Look at this car. I love **its** colour.
Regarde cette voiture. J'adore **sa** couleur.

✸ Le génitif

● On forme le génitif en ajoutant **'s** à un nom singulier et **'** à un nom pluriel. Le **'s** du génitif se prononce comme le **-s** du pluriel.

nom singulier + **'s**	pluriel en **-s** + **'**
my mother's car la voiture de ma mère	my parents' car la voiture de mes parents
John's watch la montre de John	my friends' books les livres de mes amis

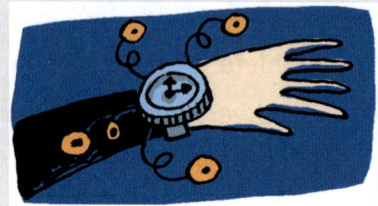

John's watch

● Le génitif sert à exprimer la possession ou un lien de parenté. L'ordre des mots est l'inverse du français.

John's computer　　　　　　　　　John's parents
l'ordinateur de John　　　　　　　　les parents de John

● Le génitif joue le même rôle que les déterminants possessifs. Il occupe donc la même place.

John's watch　　　　　　　**my mother's** car　　　　　　**my parents'** car
his watch　　　　　　　　**her** car　　　　　　　　　**their** car

Exercices

1 **Relie les mots suivants avec un génitif.**

1. Sally – hair ....

2. the Prince – house ....

3. my parents – bosses ....

4. our friends – video games ....

5. this girl – schoolbag ....

6. these girls – schoolbags ....

2 **Remplace le génitif par un déterminant possessif.**

1. Do you like <u>Snow White's</u> mother? (Blanche-Neige)

....

2. <u>Cinderella's</u> sisters are going to the ball. (Cendrillon)

....

3. Where are <u>Bluebeard's</u> keys? (Barbe-bleue)

....

4. She was <u>the Seven dwarfs'</u> friend. (les Sept Nains)

....

5. <u>Little Red Riding Hood's</u> grandparents were ill. (le Petit Chaperon rouge)

....

6. Can you imagine <u>Beauty and the Beast's</u> house? (la Belle et la Bête)

....

3 **Complète en utilisant un déterminant possessif (suivi directement du nom). Aide-toi des mots soulignés pour trouver le bon déterminant possessif.**
<u>She</u> has grey **eyes.** I like .... → I like **her** eyes.

1. <u>These kids</u> have a lot of **toys.** I like ....

2. <u>He</u> has a new **computer.** I like ....

3. <u>Camilla</u> has an old **bike.** I like ....

4. <u>This flower</u> has a strange **colour.** I like ....

4 **Complète en utilisant un génitif (suivi directement du nom). Reprends les mots soulignés.**
<u>My brother</u> has a new comic book. I borrowed .... → I borrowed my brother's comic book.

1. <u>Malika</u> has a new house. I visited ....

2. <u>John and Sandra</u> have five cousins. I know ....

3. <u>My parents</u> have a new car. I like ....

4. <u>My friend</u> collects stamps. I love looking at ....

18 Sounds, sounds, sounds... @))

1 Écoute cette comptine anglaise **(nursery rhyme)** intitulée **The lion and the unicorn.**

The lion and the unicorn

The lion and the unicorn
Were fighting for the crown;
The lion beat the unicorn
All round about the town.
Some gave them white bread,
And some gave them brown;
Some gave them plum cake,
And sent them out of town.

Associe ces mots extraits de la comptine à leur prononciation en cochant la case qui convient.

lion ☐ /ˈliɔn/ ☐ /ˈlaɪən/

unicorn ☐ /ˈjuːnɪkɔːn/ ☐ /ʌniːkɔːn/

crown ☐ /kraʊn/ ☐ /kruːn/

bread ☐ /briːd/ ☐ /bred/

> **Coup de pouce**
> Regarde la phonétique p. 4 si nécessaire.

Écoute les mots suivants et entoure l'intrus qui se prononce différemment.
crown – round – brown – plum – town – about

2 Écoute la prononciation des mots suivants d'abord seuls, puis avec un déterminant **indéfini.**
hemisphere – hour – home – hotel – house – hand – honour – human

Quels sont les deux mots dont le h ne se prononce pas ? ....

Quel déterminant les précède ? ....

3 Écoute ces mots et coche la case qui correspond à la prononciation de leur **o.**

	/əʊ/ comme dans n**o**te	/uː/ comme dans m**oo**n
old		
shoe		
know		
do		
go		
school		

4 Le démonstratif **this** (ce/cet/ceci) /ðɪs/ a une prononciation proche de sa forme plurielle **these** (ces/ceux-ci) /ðiːz/. Écoute ces phrases et dis lequel des deux a été utilisé.

1. ☐ this /ðɪs/   ☐ these /ðiːz/

2. ☐ this /ðɪs/   ☐ these /ðiːz/

3. ☐ this /ðɪs/   ☐ these /ðiːz/

4. ☐ this /ðɪs/   ☐ these /ðiːz/

5. ☐ this /ðɪs/   ☐ these /ðiːz/

Coup de pouce

Pense à t'aider du contexte, singulier ou pluriel !

5 Écoute les phrases suivantes et souligne celle où le déterminant est fortement prononcé.

1. I would like to have **a** cup of coffee.

2. Give me **the** teapot, will you?

3. He isn't just **a** singer, he is **the** best singer of **the** 21st century!

4. I don't really fancy going to **the** cinema.

5. **The** book which you lent me was one of **the** most interesting I've read so far.

6 Écoute ces mots et classe-les selon qu'ils se prononcent /ð/ ou /θ/.

Rappel
Le **th** en anglais peut se prononcer /ð/ comme dans **this** (proche du /z/) ou /θ/ comme dans **thirsty** (proche du /s/).

them – there – tooth – clothes – think – thing – thin – then – theatre – thirsty – three – Thursday – through – theirs

/ð/	/θ/

7 Classe ces mots selon la prononciation de leur voyelle.
fish – bad – rat – nine – bit – site – sit – bite – late – place – mad – thin – made – white – break – try – win – game – night

/æ/ comme dans c**a**t	/eɪ/ comme dans m**a**ke	/ɪ/ comme dans s**i**x	/aɪ/ comme dans f**i**ve

19 Les mots interrogatifs

> Les mots interrogatifs commencent par **wh-**, sauf **how**. Ils servent à poser une question sur quelqu'un, quelque chose, un moment, un lieu.

✹ Place des mots interrogatifs dans les questions

Les mots interrogatifs se placent au début de la question. Ils sont suivis d'un auxiliaire ou d'un modal.

mot interrogatif	auxiliaire / modal		
Who	is	your friend?	Qui est ton ami ?
Where	can	I go?	Où est-ce que je peux aller ?
What	is	it?	Qu'est-ce que c'est ?
Who	do	you prefer?	Qui préfères-tu ?
What	does	she want?	Qu'est-ce qu'elle veut ?
Why	does	he work so hard?	Pourquoi est-ce qu'il travaille si dur?

✹ Who? What? When? Where? Why?

who?	qui ?	**Who** can answer?	Qui peut répondre ?
what?	qu'est-ce que ? qu'est-ce qui ?	**What**'s wrong?	Qu'est-ce qui ne va pas ?
when?	quand ?	**When** are you at home?	Quand es-tu à la maison ?
where?	où ?	**Where** is she?	Où est-elle ?
why?	pourquoi ?	**Why** are they tired?	Pourquoi sont-ils fatigués ?

Note aussi comment on demande l'heure : What time is it? (Quelle heure est-il ?)

✹ Whose?

Whose correspond à « à qui ». Il est suivi directement d'un nom.

Whose bike is this?
À qui est ce vélo ?

Whose books are these?
À qui sont ces livres ?

✹ How?

● **How** s'emploie comme « comment ». Il s'emploie aussi avec un <u>adjectif</u>.

How are you feeling?
Comment te sens-tu ?

How old are you?
Quel âge as-tu ?

How tall is she?
Combien mesure-t-elle ?

● **How much** et **how many** signifient « combien ». **How many** est suivi d'un nom au <u>pluriel</u>. **How much** s'emploie seul ou suivi d'un nom au <u>singulier</u>.

How many brothers and sisters have you got?
Combien de frères et sœurs as-tu ?

How much is it?
Combien ça coûte ?

Exercices

1 **Complète ces questions par un mot interrogatif.**

1. "........................ is in the hall?" "My science teacher, Mrs Harper."
2. "........................'s that?" "It's my new electronic book."
3. "........................ are you going, Sue?" "I'm going to Chicago for the weekend."
4. "........................ time is it?" "It's midnight."
5. "........................ are you leaving, Sue?" "I'm leaving in two hours."
6. "........................ are you smiling?" "Because I got a very good mark."
7. "........................ mobile phone is this?" "It's Lenny's."

> ▪ a mark : une note

2 **Remets ces phrases dans le bon ordre. Attention aux majuscules en début de phrase.**

1. ? / are / going / you / tomorrow / where

....

2. ? / aren't / with / brother / you / your / why

....

3. ? / you / who / going / with / is

....

4. ? / yesterday / what / do / did / you

....

5. ? / Scotland / go / you / to / did / when

....

6. ? / to / school / by / go / bus / do / why / you

....

3 **Pose des questions à partir des phrases affirmatives suivantes.**
Utilise le mot interrogatif donné en amorce.
Jo likes sports. What ....? → What does Jo like?

> **Coup de pouce**
>
> Pense à l'ordre
> des mots : interrogatif
> + auxiliaire + sujet.

1. Jim is going to Japan next week. **Why** .... ?
2. Leslie loves big cities. **What** .... ?
3. His cat wakes him up at 6. **When** .... ?
4. The Walkers live in Los Angeles. **Where** .... ?
5. The Walkers are my neighbours. **Who** .... ?
6. This is Laura's bike. **Whose** .... ?
7. Naomi has got problems. **Who** .... ?

20 Trouver son chemin

@)) "Excuse me, sir, **I'm lost. Can you tell me the way to** the stadium, please? Do you know where it is?" "Sure. You're not very **far**. But the easiest way is **to take the underground.**"

« Pardon monsieur, je suis perdu. Pouvez-vous m'indiquer le chemin pour aller au stade, s'il vous plaît ? Savez-vous où il se trouve ? – Bien sûr. Vous n'êtes pas très loin. Mais le plus facile est de prendre le métro. »

✳ Lo'cating (situer)

- a place /eɪ/ : un endroit, un lieu
- here /hɪə/ : ici
- there /ðeə/ : là, là-bas
- over there /ˈəʊvə ðeə/ : là-bas
- in : dans
- on : sur
- under : sous
- in front of : devant
- behind /bɪˈhaɪnd/ : derrière
- opposite /ˈɒpəsɪt/ : en face de
- next to : à côté de
- near : près de
- between /bɪˈtwiːn/ : entre

- in'side /aɪ/ : à l'intérieur
- out'side /aɪ/ : à l'extérieur
- at the end (of) : à l'extrémité (de)
- at/on the corner : à l'angle, au coin
- around /əˈraʊnd/ here : par ici
- a street : une rue
- the traffic lights : les feux tricolores
- a 'building /ɪ/ : un bâtiment
- a shop : un magasin
- a car park : un parking
- a bus stop : un arrêt de bus
- the 'station : la gare
- a road /əʊ/ : une route

✳ Going somewhere (aller quelque part)

- this way : dans cette direction
- to the north : au nord
- to the south /saʊθ/ : au sud
- to the east /iːst/ : à l'est
- to the west : à l'ouest

- to the left : à gauche
- to the right /aɪ/ : à droite
- to turn : tourner
- straight on, straight ahead : tout droit
- to go* up a street : monter une rue
- to go* down a street : descendre une rue

on(to)	off	to	from	into	out of

✳ Asking your way (demander ton chemin)

- to be* lost : être perdu
- where : où ?
- Can you tell* me the way to...?
  Pouvez-vous m'indiquer le chemin pour... ?
- How can I get*/go* to...?
  Comment est-ce que je peux aller à... ?

- far (from) : loin (de)
- close /kləʊs/ (to) : près (de)
- to walk : aller à pied
- to take* the bus : prendre le bus
- to take* the underground : prendre le métro

1 Voici les indications que l'on t'a données pour te repérer dans le centre commercial.
Complète le plan avec le numéro correspondant à chaque lieu indiqué en gras dans les phrases
ci-dessous.

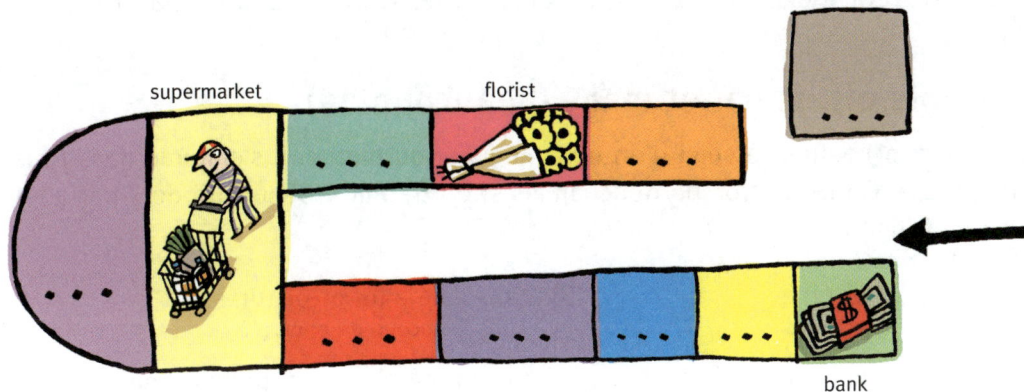

supermarket   florist

bank

1. **The cinema** is in front of the bank.

2. **The car park** is behind the supermarket.

3. **The chemist's** is next to the bank.

4. **The sports store** is opposite the florist, next to the shoe shop.

5. **The shoe shop** is next to the supermarket.

6. **The clothes shop** is between the chemist's and the sports store.

7. **The restaurant** is next to the florist. It isn't far from the cinema.

8. **The bookshop** is opposite the shoe shop.

▪ the chemist's : la pharmacie

2 Trouve le contraire des mots suivants.

1. on ≠ ....

2. in front of ≠ ....

3. inside ≠ ....

4. to the north ≠ ....

5. to the left ≠ ....

6. out of ≠ ....

7. close (to) ≠ ....

8. to go up ≠ ....

3 Associe les questions aux réponses correspondantes.

1. Can you tell me the way to the museum?

2. How far is it from here?

3. Where is it?

4. How can I get there?

● About 2 miles.

● Yes, of course, it's easy.

● You can walk up the street or take
the number 9 bus.

● In High Street, next to the town hall.

▪ the town hall : la mairie

21 A lot of, much, many, some, any et no

| Ces mots servent à exprimer une quantité. On les appelle des « quantifieurs ».

✳ A lot of (lots of), much et many (beaucoup de)

● **A lot of (lots of)** peut être suivi d'un nom singulier ou pluriel. Il s'emploie dans tous les types de phrase. On ne se trompe donc jamais si on traduit « beaucoup de » par **a lot of**.

I have **a lot of** friends.
J'ai beaucoup d'amis.

I haven't got **a lot of** time.
Je n'ai pas beaucoup de temps.

Did you take **a lot of** pictures?
Tu as pris beaucoup de photos ?

● **Much** est toujours suivi d'un nom <u>singulier</u> et **many** d'un nom <u>pluriel</u>. **Much** et **many** s'emploient surtout dans les phrases négatives et interrogatives.

I haven't got **much** time.
Je n'ai pas beaucoup de temps.

Did you take **many** pictures?
Tu as pris beaucoup de photos ?

✳ Some et any

● **Some** s'emploie surtout dans des phrases **affirmatives** pour parler d'une petite quantité. On le traduit le plus souvent par « du, de la, des ».

I would like **some** money.
Je voudrais de l'argent.

I want **some** bread, **some** jam and **some** vegetables.
Je veux du pain, de la confiture et des légumes.

● À la forme **interrogative**, on préfère utiliser **any**.

Did you buy **any** bread, or **any** jam, or **any** vegetables?
Est-ce que tu as acheté du pain, ou de la confiture, ou des légumes ?

● À la forme **négative**, on emploie **not... any**, qui correspond à « pas de ». On n'utilise pas **some** à la forme négative.

I did**n't** buy **any** bread, Jo did**n't** buy **any** jam and Lee did**n't** buy **any** vegetables!
Je n'ai pas acheté de pain, Jo n'a pas acheté de confiture et Lee n'a pas acheté de légumes !

✳ No

On peut utiliser « **no** + nom » à la place de **not... any**. Avec « **no** + nom », le verbe est à la forme affirmative.

verbe négatif + **any** + nom	verbe affirmatif + **no** + nom	
I **don't have any** money.	I **have no** money.	Je n'ai pas d'argent.
You **don't have any** friends.	You **have no** friends.	Tu n'as pas d'amis.
We **didn't buy any** stamps.	We **bought no** stamps.	Nous n'avons pas acheté de timbres.

Exercices

1 **Much** ou **many** ?

1. Are there .... stars on the American flag?

2. Kelly is sorry but she doesn't have .... time.

3. I didn't buy .... postcards.

4. Have you got .... money with you?

Dans quelles phrases peut-on utiliser **a lot of** ? ....

2 **Some** ou **any** ? Complète les phrases suivantes puis traduis les phrases ainsi obtenues.

1. We don't have .... money.

....

2. I need .... money to buy .... pens.

....

3. Did you get .... mail today?

....

4. Mike hasn't got .... friends.

....

5. Did you make .... friends during your holiday?

....

Dans quel cas as-tu choisi **some** ?

....

Pourquoi ?

....

3 Réécris ces phrases à l'aide de **no** + nom.
I haven't got any time. → I've got **no** time.

1. My cat didn't eat any vegetables.

....

2. We didn't take any pictures.

....

3. I don't have any friends.

....

4. She doesn't have any respect for my work.

....

> **Coup de pouce**
> Attention aux temps !

22 La nature

@)) A lot of National Parks in the USA offer breathtaking **landscapes.** In Death Valley National Park, CA, you will be in a **stony** desert, whereas in Yosemite, you will hike in the **mountains,** you will cross **streams** and **waterfalls.**

Beaucoup de parcs nationaux aux États-Unis offrent des paysages à couper le souffle. Dans le parc national de la Vallée de la Mort, en Californie, vous serez dans un désert de pierre, alors qu'à Yosemite, vous randonnerez dans les montagnes, vous traverserez des ruisseaux et des cascades !

✹ At the 'seaside (au bord de la mer)

- water : l'eau
- the sea : la mer
- a wave : une vague
- the tide /taɪd/ : la marée
- a 'lighthouse : un phare
- land : la terre
- an island /'aɪlənd/ : une île

- the coast /kəʊst/ : la côte
- the shore : le rivage
- a cliff : une falaise
- a port, a harbour : un port
- a beach /iː/ : une plage
- sand : du sable

✹ In the countryside (à la campagne)

- the country /'kʌntri/ : la campagne
- the landscape : le paysage
- a village : un village
- a field /iː/ : un champ
- the crops : les cultures
- wheat /iː/ : le blé
- a hill : une colline
- a hedge : une haie
- a bush /ʊ/ : un buisson
- grass : de l'herbe
- a flower : une fleur

- a 'forest : une forêt
- a wood : un bois
- a tree : un arbre
- a branch : une branche
- a leaf (pl. leaves) : une feuille
- an oak : un chêne
- a chestnut tree : un châtaignier
- a 'river /ɪ/ : une rivière
- a lake : un lac
- a moor : une lande
- heather /e/ : la bruyère

✹ In the mountains (à la montagne)

- a mountain /'maʊntɪn/ : une montagne
- a range /eɪ/ : une chaîne de montagnes
- a plateau : un plateau
- a valley /i/ : une vallée
- a stream /iː/ : un ruisseau
- a 'waterfall : une cascade

- a fir /ɜː/ : un sapin
- a cave /eɪ/ : une grotte
- a refuge : un refuge [de montagne]
- rock : de la roche
- a stone : une pierre
- stony : de pierre

Exercices

1 Complète cette description du dessin.

This picture represents a village
at the foot of a ....,
on top of which there is a yellow

....
It is on a small ....
There is a ....
.... where people can
bathe in summer.

- to bathe : se baigner

2 Fais correspondre ces noms aux types de paysages auxquels ils se rattachent.

1. heather
2. a hill
3. water
4. sand
5. a fir

● the countryside
● a lake
● the mountain
● a moor
● a beach

3 Trouve dans la grille la traduction des mots suivants. Avec les lettres qui restent, tu formeras un mot qui te dira de quoi sont faites les montagnes.

phare – buisson – eau – blé – plage – bois – haie – chêne – mer – herbe – feuille

L	I	G	H	T	H	O	U	S	E
O	A	K	C	L	E	A	F	S	W
W	H	E	A	T	D	S	O	A	O
W	A	T	E	R	G	E	R	R	O
H	S	U	B	C	E	A	K	G	D

Coup de pouce

Les mots peuvent se lire dans tous les sens.

Mot mystère : __ __ __ __

4 Trouve les mots correspondant aux définitions suivantes.

1. There are many in a tree: ....

2. There are many on a branch: ....

3. Ness in Scotland is one: ....

4. The Thames is one: ....

5. At the seaside it can be high or low: ....

6. You may grill its fruit in October: ....

23 Les prépositions et les particules

En anglais, comme en français, on doit parfois utiliser une préposition entre le verbe et son complément. La particule est un petit mot qui ressemble à une préposition. Mais elle fait partie du verbe et en change le sens.

✷ Les verbes suivis d'une préposition

● Voici quelques verbes + préposition à retenir.

belong to sb
appartenir à qqn

look after sth/sb
s'occuper de qqch./qqn

think of (ou about) sth/sb
penser à qqch./qqn

dream of sth/sb
rêver de qqch./qqn

speak, talk about sth/sb
parler de qqch./qqn

translate into English
traduire en anglais

be sorry about sth
être désolé, s'excuser de qqch.

thank sb for sth
remercier qqn pour qqch.

write to sb
écrire à qqn

● Parfois, on trouve une préposition en anglais mais pas en français.

ask for sth
demander qqch.

look for sth/sb
chercher qqch./qqn

pay for sth
payer qqch.

look at sth/sb
regarder qqch./qqn

listen to sth/sb
écouter qqch./qqn

wait for sth/sb
attendre qqch./qqn

● Mais on n'emploie pas de préposition avec **enter** (entrer dans), **obey** (obéir à), **remember** (se souvenir de) et **trust** (faire confiance à).

They did not **enter** the classroom.
Ils ne sont pas entrés dans la salle de cours.

This dog does not **obey** its owners.
Ce chien n'obéit pas à ses maîtres.

Do you **remember** Mrs Ahmed?
Tu te souviens de Madame Ahmed ?

✷ Les verbes suivis d'une particule

● Certains verbes sont composés de deux mots. Le premier mot est le verbe proprement dit, qui se conjugue. Le second est un petit mot qu'on appelle « particule ». La particule accompagne toujours le verbe !

Stand up!
Lève-toi !

Sit down!
Assieds-toi !

● Voici quelques verbes à particule.

verbe simple	verbe à particule	verbe simple	verbe à particule
bring (apporter)	bring up sb (élever qqn)	go (aller)	go on (continuer)
call (appeler)	call back (rappeler)	look (regarder)	look up (lever les yeux)
come (venir)	come in (entrer)	sit (être assis)	sit down (s'asseoir)
get (obtenir)	get up (se lever) [d'un lit]	stand (être debout)	stand up (se lever)
give (donner)	give up (abandonner)	take (prendre)	take off (décoller) [avion]

Exercices

1 Utilise la préposition qui convient : **to, for, at** ou **about**.

1. I love looking .... the moon. (regarder)

2. I'm looking .... my keys. (chercher)

3. Does this house belong .... your parents? (appartenir à)

4. I'm not talking .... you. (parler à)

5. I'm talking .... Rhoda. (parler de)

6. They are looking .... a new apartment. (chercher)

7. How much did you pay .... this software? (payer)

2 Complète ces phrases. Attention, parfois il ne faut rien mettre!

1. I'm waiting .... the train to Glasgow.

2. What are you thinking .... ?

3. Rex always obeys .... my sister, not me.

4. We're writing a letter .... Grandma.

5. I don't remember .... your cousin. Do I know him?

6. We entered .... the house in silence.

7. I trust .... every person I meet.

3 Remets ces questions dans le bon ordre. Attention : la préposition se place à la fin de la question.

1. ? / you / waiting / are / for / who

....

2. ? / is / what / Luke / about / thinking

....

3. ? / who / Martha / to / talking / is

....

4. ? / are / the / writing / on / what / pupils

....

4 Dis si le mot souligné est une préposition ou une particule.

1. Don't give <u>up</u> the fight! ....

2. Give this letter <u>to</u> her. ....

3. The cat is sleeping <u>on</u> my bed. ....

4. You should go <u>on</u>. ....

▪ the fight : le combat

1 Lucy sort de la gare (**station**) et cherche à aller au musée. Écoute les instructions et dis à quel bâtiment du plan le musée correspond : A, B, C ou D.

Le musée correspond à la lettre

....

2 Écoute les mots suivants et souligne la syllabe accentuée.

phonetic	scientific	exotic	academic
optimistic	sarcastic	organic	synthetic
historical	practical	illogical	identical

Où se situe à chaque fois la syllabe accentuée par rapport au suffixe **-ic** ? ....

3 Dans les questions suivantes, note si l'intonation est montante (↗) ou descendante (↘) en fin de phrase.

1. How many biscuits do you want? ☐ ↗ ☐ ↘

2. Where does your sister live? ☐ ↗ ☐ ↘

3. Are you busy right now? ☐ ↗ ☐ ↘

4. Can anybody help me? ☐ ↗ ☐ ↘

5. Who is your favourite singer? ☐ ↗ ☐ ↘

6. Is he going to move to Australia? ☐ ↗ ☐ ↘

7. Who is your source of inspiration? ☐ ↗ ☐ ↘

Que remarques-tu ?

Quand la question commence par un pronom interrogatif (**how, where...**),

l'intonation est ....

Quand elle commence par un auxiliaire, elle est ....

4 Écoute ces phrases et choisis l'expression donnée par leur intonation.

1. Why can't you forget him?
☐ surprise   ☐ irritation   ☐ curiosité

2. Why can't you forget him?
☐ surprise   ☐ irritation   ☐ curiosité

3. You'd better not use a dictionary for this translation.
☐ ton autoritaire   ☐ bienveillance   ☐ colère

4. You'd better not use a dictionary for this translation.
☐ ton autoritaire   ☐ bienveillance   ☐ colère

5. My brother is supposed to stay at home during the holidays.
☐ joie   ☐ énervement   ☐ tristesse

6. My brother is supposed to stay at home during the holidays.
☐ joie   ☐ énervement   ☐ tristesse

5 Dans les paires suivantes, souligne le mot dont la voyelle est longue.

sit – seat   bird – bed   bean – bin   bun – burn   read – rid

far – fat   still – steal   black – blue   pot – port   gin – jeans

6 Certains mots s'écrivent presque de la même façon en anglais et en français. Écoute les mots suivants, écris-les d'abord en anglais puis note la lettre du dessin correspondant.

 a
 b
 c
 d

 e
 f
 g
 h

1. ....   **5.** ....

2. ....   **6.** ....

3. ....   **7.** ....

4. ....   **8.** ....

Coup de pouce Les mots sont dits dans le désordre.

Verbes irréguliers

infinitif	prétérit	part. passé	sens	infinitif	prétérit	part. passé	sens
be	was, were	been	*être*	**learn**	learned, learnt	learned, learnt	*apprendre*
beat	beat	beaten	*battre*				
become	became	become	*devenir*	**leave**	left	left	*quitter*
begin	began	begun	*commencer*	**lose** /uː/	lost /ɒ/	lost /ɒ/	*perdre*
break	broke	broken	*casser*	**make**	made	made	*faire*
bring	brought	brought	*apporter*	**mean** /iː/	meant /e/	meant /e/	*vouloir dire*
build /ɪ/	built	built	*construire*	**meet** /iː/	met /e/	met /e/	*rencontrer*
buy	bought	bought	*acheter*	**pay**	paid	paid	*payer*
catch	caught	caught	*attraper*	**put**	put	put	*poser*
choose /uː/	chose /əʊ/	chosen /əʊ/	*choisir*	**read** /iː/	read /e/	read /e/	*lire*
come	came	come	*venir*	**ride**	rode	ridden	*aller [à vélo, à cheval]*
cost	cost	cost	*coûter*				
cut	cut	cut	*couper*	**run**	ran	run	*courir*
do	did	done	*faire*	**say** /eɪ/	said /e/	said /e/	*dire*
draw	drew	drawn	*dessiner / tirer*	**see**	saw	seen	*voir*
				sell	sold	sold	*vendre*
dream /iː/	dreamed, dreamt /e/	dreamed, dreamt /e/	*rêver*	**send**	sent	sent	*envoyer*
				set	set	set	*placer, fixer*
drink	drank	drunk	*boire*	**show**	showed	shown	*montrer*
drive /aɪ/	drove	driven /ɪ/	*conduire*	**sing**	sang	sung	*chanter*
eat	ate /eɪ/	eaten	*manger*	**sit**	sat	sat	*être assis*
fall	fell	fallen	*tomber*	**sleep** /iː/	slept /e/	slept /e/	*dormir*
feel	felt	felt	*(se) sentir*	**speak**	spoke	spoken	*parler*
fight /aɪ/	fought /ɔː/	fought	*combattre*	**spend**	spent	spent	*passer / dépenser*
find	found	found	*trouver*				
fly	flew	flown	*voler [avec des ailes]*	**stand**	stood	stood	*être debout*
				steal	stole	stolen	*voler, dérober*
forget	forgot	forgotten	*oublier*				
get	got	got / gotten (US)	*obtenir*	**swim**	swam	swum	*nager*
				take	took	taken	*prendre*
give	gave	given	*donner*	**teach**	taught	taught	*enseigner*
go	went	gone	*aller*	**tell**	told	told	*dire / raconter*
grow	grew	grown	*pousser*				
have	had	had	*avoir*	**think**	thought	thought	*penser*
hear /ɪə/	heard /ɜː/	heard /ɜː/	*entendre*	**throw** /əʊ/	threw /uː/	thrown /əʊ/	*lancer*
hide /aɪ/	hid /ɪ/	hidden /ɪ/	*cacher*	**understand**	understood	understood	*comprendre*
hit	hit	hit	*frapper*	**wake up**	waked up, woke up	waked up, woken up	*réveiller*
hold /əʊ/	held	held	*tenir*				
hurt /ɜː/	hurt	hurt	*faire mal*	**wear** /eə/	wore	worn	*porter [vêtement]*
keep	kept	kept	*garder*				
know /nəʊ/	knew /njuː/	known	*savoir / connaître*	**weep**	wept	wept	*pleurer*
				win	won /ʌ/	won /ʌ/	*gagner*
				write /raɪt/	wrote /rəʊt/	written /rɪtən/	*écrire*

Index

s'engage pour
l'environnement en réduisant
l'empreinte carbone de ses livres.
Celle de cet exemplaire est de :
500 g éq. CO_2
Rendez-vous sur
www.hatier-durable.fr

Achevé d'imprimer par l'Imprimerie de Champagne à Langres — France
Dépôt légal : 99166-0/02 — Octobre 2016